Unfolding the Arab-Israeli Conflict

1894-1970

by

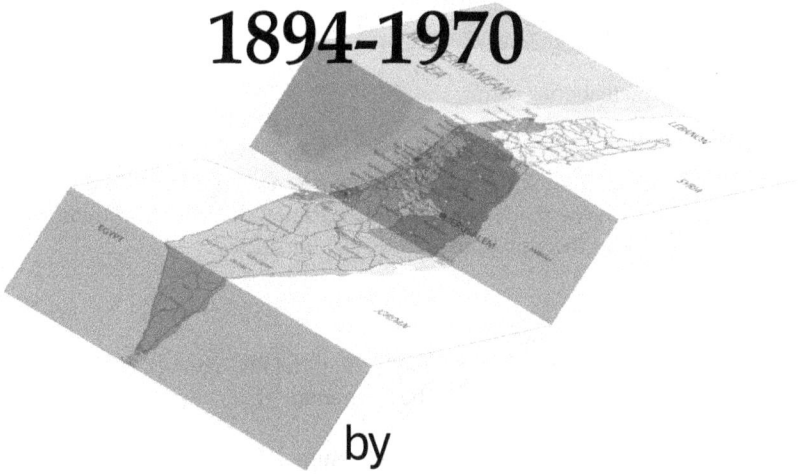

Muhammad Hallaj

Sage Tea Books
Purcellville, Virginia

Sage Tea Books
P. O. Box 456
Purcellville, VA 20134
www.sageteabooks.com

Publisher's Note: Although the author is no longer with us, his heirs and publishers have made only minor editorial changes. The experiences, the research, and the words are all those of the author.

Ordering Information:
Quantity discounts are available. For details, contact the "Special Sales Department" at the address above or email dixiehallaj@gmail.com.

Unfolding the Arab-Israeli Conflict/Muhammad Hallaj
History, Middle East, Palestine, Arab-Israeli Conflict
ISBN 978-1-63320-083-8 Paperback Edition
ISBN 978-1-63320-084-5 Ebook Edition
ISBN 978-1-63320-085-2 Audio Edition
ISBN 978-1-63320-086-9 Hardback Edition

To those who gave their lives protecting
PALESTINE
and to those who hope to have a part in
the rebuilding.

UNFOLDING THE ARAB-ISRAELI CONFLICT

TABLE OF CONTENTS

EDITOR'S PREFACE

In *Unfolding the Arab-Israeli Conflict,* Dr. Muhammad Hallaj brings a unique perspective to the Arab-Israeli Conflict. Born in mandated Palestine, he witnessed the violent results of the plan to partition his small country of Palestine into two even smaller entities. He lived and worked under military occupation, and he was a member of the Palestine National Council during the abortive peace process that resulted in the Oslo Accords. With a Ph.D. in Political Science (International Relations), he brings both the experiential and the scholarly credentials to bear on the topic.

The peppering of very personal views and experiences bring the conflict into the real world for the reader with little or no knowledge of the subject, while his use of references from U.N. observers will interest even the most knowledgeable reader.

Hallaj's observations are backed by a lifetime of study and reflection, and they are as relevant today as they were when he began writing *Unfolding the Arab-Israeli Conflict.* The fact that the Question of Palestine continues to exist and continues to claim lives, now measured in the tens of thousands, is proof that the problem is complex and there is no quick fix. A greater effort is needed and a thorough understanding of the root of the problem is required. Unless the problem is solved, it will continue to flare up in ever-escalating conflicts that threaten to spread into ever-widening battlefields.

PART I

PLANTING THE SEEDS

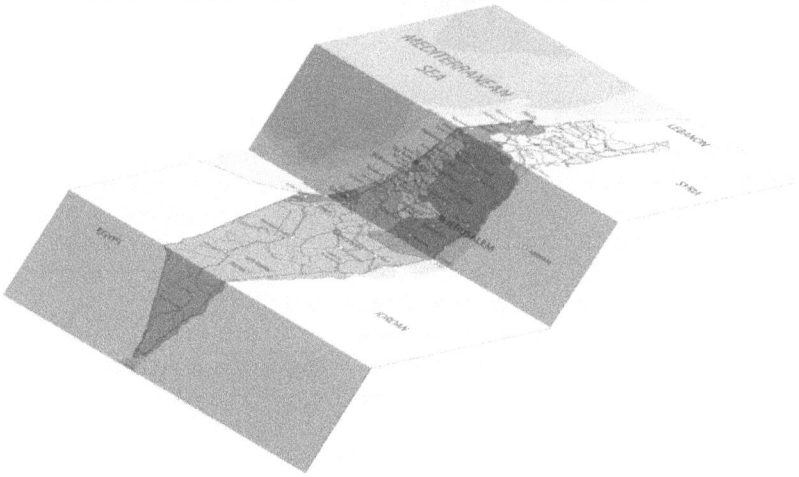

CHAPTER 1- INTRODUCTION

Once upon a time a French general fell off his horse and broke his leg. Doctors rushed to his side and devoted themselves to mending it. Their devotion to this task was so complete they failed to notice that the general was dying from an acute attack of appendicitis until it was too late. Unfortunately, this type of incident is often encountered in international politics. Our preoccupation with the potentially disastrous clash between the superpowers is of course understandable, but such preoccupation often blinds us to the fact that there are other problems and grievances which demand urgent attention. Some of these problems have the disappointing tendency not to vanish when they are ignored. On the contrary, they tend to feed and grow on negligence. One such problem is that of Palestine.

Since the United Nations General Assembly recommended the partition of Palestine into Arab and Jewish states on November 29, 1947, the Holy Land has been the scene of continuous strife. The armed conflict which resulted from the attempt to partition the country was *suspended* by the Armistice Agreements of 1949. These agreements had been envisioned as temporary arrangements pending the attainment of permanent peace. Not only have the Armistice Agreements been riddled with serious violations, but they've also failed to bring the anticipated peace one step closer to reality than it had ever been.

The Israelis and their supporters accuse the Arabs of preparing to push the Jews into the sea. The Arabs and their supporters reply that the Israelis have already pushed a million[1] Palestinian Arabs out of their homes into a sea of suffering and bitterness.

The rest of the world casually delivers to both sides a love-thy-neighbor sermon the moral of which is that if the Arabs and the Jews only will it, there would be peace in Palestine. This attitude of peace-by-will-power is based on the assumption that the Palestine problem was *solved* when the country was partitioned. Those who hold this view attribute time the miraculous power to heal all wounds. They assert that, given sufficient time, the tempers of the Arabs and their Jewish cousins would adequately subside to make them see clearly that "what is, is right," or acceptable at any rate. Unfortunately, time is not the healer of all wounds. The fact that the Palestine problem is not, nor has it ever been, the product of petulance renders it quite resistance to time therapy.

Meanwhile, the problem continues to worsen. As time goes on, both adversaries increase their destructive capabilities, quantitatively and qualitatively. And now, we have reached the point where nuclear weapons have in all probability been introduced in the Middle East. Moreover, the major powers become more and more

---

1 Editor's Note: This manuscript was completed before the 2023-2024 hostilities in Gaza, which has since raised the number of Palestinians driven from their homes to more than three million.

involved in the Arab-Israeli quarrel and the chances become greater that the next Arab Israeli confrontation may escalate into World War III.

In attempting to ascertain the reasons for the failure of peace to "break out" in Palestine, it is useless to look for these reasons in an answer to the question of what went wrong with the "solution" of Palestine's problem, because *nothing went wrong with partition.* By causing so much suffering and by failing to result in peace, the partition of Palestine is running true to form — it is being itself, a cause for suffering and an impediment to peace.

The thesis of this book is that the Arab-Israeli conflict is irreconcilable, and thus is not amenable to peaceful settlement *on the basis of the status quo.* Moreover, the conflict is too dynamic to permit it to be merely an irritation which, nevertheless, one can become accustomed to living with. The Arab-Israeli conflict to say the same thing in a different way, can neither be placated nor ignored. Therefore, a policy aimed at perpetuating the status quo in Palestine *necessarily* perpetuates the recurrence of violent outbreaks. The status quo cannot serve as a basis for a peaceful and permanent solution of the problem.

Before the validity of this assertion can be demonstrated the nature of the problem which brought about the conflict must be stated. This statement is not found to be necessary because of a lack of "histories" of the Palestine problem, but because a maze of myths has been woven around it which makes it seem to be what it is not. Moreover, since this book attempts to demonstrate that the partitioning of Palestine did not and could not

3

solve the Palestine problem, it is necessary to define what that problem was.

CHAPTER 2 - ZIONISM

Eight miles off the coast of French Guiana, there protrudes out of the depths of the South Atlantic a sixteen-square-mile dry, sandy, and torrid rock formation appropriately called Devil's Island. This island, whose climatic conditions are said to be so unsuited for human life that confinement to it is tantamount to a sentence of death by torture, was used by the French government as a penal colony until its abandonment shortly after World War II. More than half a century before the inhumanity of the practice finally dawned upon the governors of the Land of Enlightenment, an ex-captain, Alfred Dreyfus by name, who had been convicted for treason by a unanimous French military court on December 22, 1894, was sentenced to life on Devil's Island. The island never promised anything but intolerable torment to its inmates, and to captain Dreyfus it promised to be doubly so, because he had been convicted for a crime of which he was innocent.

The evidence against the accused captain consisted of an unsigned letter to the German military attaché in Paris, which was stolen from the German embassy by a French agent. The letter clearly indicated that its writer was spying for the Germans, because it stated that he was planning to deliver certain French military documents to them. The handwriting resembled that of Dreyfus, but it was not definitely established to be his,[2] and he was convicted in a highly irregular manner. The conviction was clearly a miscarriage of justice. This fact, however, was not obvious to the French public at the time because the French general staff repeatedly asserted that they possessed conclusive documentary evidence of Dreyfus's guilt, but that the evidence could not be revealed, because that might lead to war with Germany since the Kaiser was personally involved.[3]

In addition to this supposed need for secrecy, there were at least two other factors which might have militated against a fair trial for the accused. The first factor was the fact that the trial took place at a time when France's desire to avenge her defeat at the hands of Germany in 1870 was nothing less than a national obsession. France was to vindicate herself, and the Army was to do it for her. Consequently, the army became France's hope — or so it seemed — for the restoration of her honor, France's way to salvation. A few souls believed in Dreyfus's innocence and had the courage to say so, but this amounted to saying that the French Army and its General Staff were incompetent. "Patriotic" Frenchmen resented this attack on the Army, the instrument through which their hope for a future deliverance of their country was to be fulfilled and rose to defend it against its assailants. This they did by refusing to believe that the army was unable to detect

---

[2] Graphologists gave conflicting opinions.
[3] Years later, these documents were shown to have been forgeries.

the real offender and was, instead, prosecuting an innocent man.

The second factor which might have militated against a fair trial even at the expense of the army's reputation was the fact that the accused was both an Alsatian and a member of a minority group. Alfred Dreyfus was a French Jew. The Third Republic was going through one of the shakier phases of its unstable career, and its enemies — who not only yearned but also worked for the restoration of the "good old" pre-Republican days — saw in the fact that the "traitor" belonged to a minority group a God-given opportunity to make the life of the Republic utterly miserable. This they attempted to do by activating in their countrymen that part of man which is more easily accessible to emotion than to reason: prejudice. Anti-minority-ism (which when directed against Jews is misnamed anti-Semitism)[4] became a feature of the Dreyfus affair, and France witnessed one of the least tolerant moments in her republican history. Newspaper editors explained that Dreyfus's treason showed that a Jew was incapable of being a good Frenchman, and that even French Protestants were more loyal to Germany, the mortal foe, than to France.[5] Senator Scheurer-Kestner, a Protestant who was the president of the French Senate, hinted that he believed in Dreyfus's innocence, whereupon some papers "advised the senator

---

[4] Presumably the term anti-Semitism may be understood to describe an attitude toward all Semitic people, and not just the Jews. But the term anti-Semitism will be used here as it is generally used.

[5] This accusation was prompted by the fact that the Dreyfus supporters included many prominent French Protestants.

7

to take his seat in the Prussian Parliament"[6] where he presumably belonged. In short, the France which tried Captain Dreyfus was the aroused France of *la revanche*, the intolerant France which Émile Zola had to flee.

At the time of the Dreyfus trial, a Jewish reporter from Vienna was working as the Paris correspondent of the *Neue Freie Presse*, an Austrian newspaper, and it was in that capacity that he walked into the courtroom to cover the trial for his newspaper. After his conviction, Captain Dreyfus was degraded in public, and the watching crowd shouted their approval. "Down with the Jews!" The Jewish reporter, whose name was Theodore Herzl, watched this ceremony, listened to the crowd, and the creed of despair began to crystallize within his mind. This creed of despair was Zionism.

"I have been since youth a writer and a journalist, with no thought of the Jews," Herzl recorded in his diary a few months after Dreyfus's conviction. "But my experiences and observations and the growing pressure of anti-Semitism have forced me to the [Jewish} problem."[7]

To Herzl, Dreyfus's conviction was more than a miscarriage of justice; it represented "the desire of the vast majority of the French to condemn a Jew, and to condemn

---

[6] For some of the more recent accounts of the Dreyfus affair see Nicholas Halasz, *Captain Dreyfus: The Story of a Mass Hysteria* (New York: Grove Press, 1955); Barbara W. Tuchman, *The Proud Tower* (New York: Macmillan, 1966); Leslie Derfler, *The Dreyfus Affair: Tragedy of Errors?* (Boston: D.C. Heath and Co., 1963); H. R. Kedward, *The Dreyfus Affair: Catalyst for Tensions in French Society* (London: Longmans, Green, and Co., Ltd., 1965).

[7] *The Diaries of Theodor Herzl*, ed. and tr. By Marvin Lowenthal. (New York: The Dial Press, 1956), P. 15.

all Jews in this one Jew."[8] nor was this desire to "burn the Jews" limited to Frenchmen, Herzl thought, because "the countries in whose midst Jews live are all either covertly or openly anti-Semitic."[9] Moreover, Herzl was convinced that anti-Semitism was increasing "day by day and hour by hour" and that it was "bound to increase."[10] Granting the rights of citizenship to Jews was not an adequate protection against gentile intolerance. On the contrary, Herzl wrote, "anti-Semitism is a consequence of the emancipation of the Jews,"[11] because "the very impossibility of getting at the Jews nourishes and embitters hatred of them."[12]

In the fashion of a much older era, when the world was said to have been divided into Greeks and Barbarians, Herzl saw the human race as a polarized society consisting of two antagonistic groups: Jews and anti-Semites. Herzl even banished the assimilated prosperous Jews to the anti-Semitic camp. He explained that this group of Jews organized philanthropies and financed the emigration of "wandering Jews" to "dispatch these poor creatures just as fast and far as possible. And thus, many an apparent friend of the Jews turns out, on careful inspection, to be nothing more than an anti-Semite of Jewish origin, disguised as a philanthropist."[13]

---

[8] Theodor Herzl, *The Jewish State.* (New York: American Zionist Emergecy Council, 1946), p. 34.

[9] *Ibid.,* p. 86.

[10] *Ibid.,* p. 91.

[11] Herzl, *Diaries,* p. 9.

[12] Herzl, The Jewish State, p. 90.

[13] *Ibid.,* p. 81.

Starting with these views, Herzl moved on to seek a solution to the "Jewish problem period." It occurred to him that a solution might be found in a wholesale conversion of Jews to Christianity. Herzl had an elaborate procedure worked out by which he and other Jewish leaders would lead the Jews to the churches, and, at the appointed hour, church bells would start ringing, the Jews would go in and be baptized, and the leaders would go away to be the last generation of Jews.[14] He was serious enough about this idea to talk it over with his Jewish colleagues on the *Neue Freie Presse*, but they dissuaded him from trying to follow the plan through, and it was discarded.

Finally, Herzl, who thought he was an inspired man[15], reached the conclusion that the Jews were not only members of a religious community which belonged to diverse nationalities but members of a scattered nation which was spending its life "in exile." This Jewish nation has been subjected to political economic and social restrictions throughout the Christian era. What the Jews really needed, thought Herzl, was a territory, any territory, where they could be fenced in with a charter or a declaration of independence, and where they could have "hooked noses, black or red beards, and bandy legs, without being despised for it."[16]

---

[14] Herzl, Diaries. pp 7-8.

[15] "Am I working the plan out?" he asked himself, and then answered: "No, it is working itself out through me...This is what used to be called 'inspiration.'" Herzl, *Diaries*, p. 45.

[16] *Ibid.* p. 46.

This was the essence of Zionism, the creed of despair which began to materialize in Herzl's mind as he watched the public degradation of Captain Alfred Dreyfus.[17]

Zionist writers have attempted, with considerable success, to present their creed in nobler and a more touching manner. They portrayed it as the age-old yearning of an "exiled" people to "return to their ancient home." In order to do this, they have exploited biblical references to the history of Palestine in such a way as to implant in the public mind, especially in Christian countries, an identification of the history of Palestine with the history of the Jews. The Bible lends itself to this type of exploitation because it is concerned only with the interval which coincided with the presence of the Jewish people in the Holy Land. This relatively short interval in Palestine's history is made to appear as if it were *the* history of Palestine.

The other method which Zionist writers used to give their creed a more favorable public image was to discount the importance of anti-Semitism as the root of the Zionist movement. Thus, in his "Introduction" to Theodor Herzl's *Diaries*, Marvin Lowenthal wrote: "Even though Herzl

---

[17] In 1894, it is interesting t Jews o note, Herzl came across the Zionist solution and definitely rejected it. Discussing the novel *Femme de Claude*, by Dumas the younger, he says of one of its characters: "The good Jew Daniel wants to rediscover the homeland of his race and gather his scattered brothers into it. But a man like Daniel would surely know that *the historic homeland of the Jews* no longer has any value for them. It is childish to go in search of the geographic location of this homeland. And if the Jews really 'return home' one day, they would discover on the next day that they do not belong together. For centuries they have been rooted in diverse nationalities." Quoted in Alex Bein, "Biography," in Herzl, *The Jewish State,* pp. 31-32.

11

expressly stated in 1899 that the Dreyfus case had made him a Zionist, it was at best an appropriate myth, a dramatic foreshortening of the facts."[18] It is obvious, however, from the preceding paragraphs and from innumerable entries in his diary that Herzl's "Jewish nationalism" was entirely due to anti-Semitism and was merely a reaction to it. When he confided to his diary on July 6th, 1895, the gist of a conversation with a coreligionist of his by saying: "Nordau and I agreed…that only anti-Semitism had made Jews of us,"[19] Herzl was reiterating a conviction which permeates his writings.

Herzl was aware of the fact that the "age-old yearning for the homeland" was largely a myth. He believed that the Jews "shall have to sink still lower, we shall have to be more widely insulted, spat upon, mocked, beaten, robbed and slain before we are ripe for the idea [of a Jewish state]."[20] Herzl was hopeful, however, that "anti-Semites [will] provide the requisite impetus."[21]

Even after "returning" to the "homeland," Herzl believed, the Jews would have to be somehow persuaded to stay. He was afraid that "Vienna cafes" might have a stronger claim on his people's loyalty than the "ancient homeland." So, he decided to take the cafes along. "I shall transport over there genuine Vienna cafes," Herzl wrote. "With these small expedients, I ensure the desirable illusion of the old environment."[22] Obviously, this

---

[18] Herzl, *Diaries*, p. xix.
[19] *Ibid.*, p. 56.
[20] *Ibid.*, p. 25.
[21] Herzl, The Jewish State, p. 129.
[22] Herzl, *Diaries*, p. 41.

indicates that the Zionist's contention that their creed was a manifestation of the ancient desire of the Jewish people to "return to their historical homeland" was a misrepresentation of facts.

This statement, of course, is not meant to discount the significance of Palestine as a land holy to Judaism as it is to Christianity and to Islam. It is merely intended to point out the fact that Zionism exploited a religious sentiment for the advancement of a political goal, an act which was resented and opposed by religious Jews even before the Palestinian Arabs had heard of Zionism or had become aware of its threat to their homeland.

This was clearly indicated by the fact that the most considerable and persistent opposition to Zionism among the Jews emanated—as it still does—from the religious Jews.[23] These groups had traditionally looked upon the "return" of the Jews to Palestine "not as a simple historic or human event, but as part of the divine scheme of governance... Any attempt to further that consummation by human beings and in human fashion... Would have appeared to be blasphemy, and attempt at terrestrial interference with the divine process."[24]

To religious Jews, in other words, the Zionists' political aims and methods amounted to a denial of [or a disbelief in] a central Judaic tenet. This Jewish opposition to the concept of "Jewish nationalism" was more dramatically expressed by the removal of "all mention of

---

[23] For example, the American Council for Judaism.
[24] Richard J. H. Gottheil, *Zionism*. (Philadelphia: The Jewish Publication Society of America, 1939), pp. 35-36.

Zion and Jerusalem from the official prayer book" by the Advanced Jewish Reform communities in Germany and in America.[25]

Other non- Zionist Jews took the position that "the role of the Jews lies in the very opposite direction of that preached by Zionism."[26] they believed that the dispersion of the Jews was more conductive to the fulfillment of their mission of spreading the "true" monotheistic religion. Other Jews still opposed Zionism on secular grounds. The Central Conference of American Rabbis declared that the Zionist claim that all Jews belonged to an "exiled" stateless nation does "not benefit, but infinitely harm, our Jewish brethren where they are still persecuted, by confirming the assertion of their enemies that the Jews are foreigners in the countries in which they are at home."[27]

Zionism is not Judaism, and if the distinction and even the conflict between them is not made, no clear understanding of the Zionist movement can be obtained. This confusion of Zionism with Judaism has been encouraged by the Zionists who used the words "Jew" and "Zionist" as if they were synonymous and interchangeable.

In his 1896 booklet, *The Jewish State,* Herzl propounded his above-mentioned views on anti-Semitism and advocated the establishment of a Jewish state as a solution to the Jewish problem. Herzl's ideas expounded in *The Jewish State* were not entirely new.

---

[25] *Ibid,* pp. 99-100.
[26] *Ibid.*
[27] *Ibid.,* p. 102.

Before the Dreyfus case made Herzl aware of the existence of a Jewish problem, Jewish and non-Jewish writers had lamented the intolerance of the human race and adopted various remedies. But whereas previous attempts to solve the Jewish problem were mainly restricted to philanthropic undertakings designed to facilitate the migration and resettlement of Jews, Herzl converted Zionism into a world movement oriented toward political action.[28]

In 1897, Herzl established and became the first president of the World Zionist Organization. This Organization assumed the task of mobilizing world Jewry for the purpose of executing Herzl's proposed solution to the Jewish problem: to find, with the help and under the protection of a great power, a territory upon which a Jewish state could be established.

Argentina and Palestine were two possibilities which suggested themselves to Herzl. Argentina, where some Jewish settlements had already been set up, could be persuaded to sell a part of its territory—Herzl thought—upon which the Zionist would "ingather" the Jews and set up their state.

Palestine held no special attraction for the Zionist leader. He merely looked upon it as "one of the various possibilities for Jewish settlement, as is Argentina or

---

[28] This chapter deals only with Herzl's (political) Zionism because it is the most relevant to the subject of this book. It is the most relevant because it was the ideological basis on which the World Zionist Organization was built, and which came to dominate the Zionist movement and its goal of establishing a Jewish state in Palestine.

Canada."[29] even as one of various possibilities, he found Palestine to compare unfavorably. While finding many faults with Palestine, he could think of only one advantage, and that advantage turned out to be a legend. "Against Palestine," Herzl wrote in his diary on June 9, 1895, "is its proximity to Russia and to Europe, its small size, as well as its unaccustomed climate. In its favor, the mighty legend."[30] The Russian Jews, on the other hand, insisted on Palestine. Unlike Argentina, Palestine was not an independent country and that would make it easier to obtain because it could be bought from the Turkish despot of whose empire Palestine had the misfortune to be a part. Its people lacked the political means of its defense.

Representing the Zionist Organization, Herzl began to negotiate with Turkey. He bribed his way into an audience with the Turkish Sultan,[31] and put before him the Zionist offer.

---

[29] Gottheil, *Zionism*, p. 91.

[30] Herzl, *Diaries*, pp. 40-41. The "mighty legend" obviously is a reference to the "return" of the Jews to Palestine.

[31] Herzl, *Diaries*. Sections dealing with negotiations with Turkey. Evidently, Herzl did not hesitate to use whatever means were promised to promote his ends. He did not even rule out the resort to demagoguery. "Jews," he wrote, "are hungry for KOVED—honor and attention—being a despised people, and by catering to it one can lead them." (p. 57). Under another entry in his diary, Herzl revealed the method he would use against the Jewish Baron de Hirsch, should the latter dare to divulge the content of certain letters which Herzl had sent him, which contained unflattering observations on the personality of the Jewish people. Herzl wrote: " I am not afraid of his divulging my three letters. I should only reply by smashing him—inflaming popular fanaticism against him and demolishing him in print." (p. 35).

Turkey had assumed a burdensome external national debt which its creditor European powers were using as a pretext for intervention in the affairs of the Ottoman Empire. The Zionists offered to raise enough money to loan to Turkey for the purpose of paying its debt, and Palestine was to be the pound of flesh which the Zionists demanded for this service to the Sultan.[32]

In order to render Turkey dependent upon Zionist financial aid and to force it to deal with them, the Zionists sought to block Turkey's chances of securing loans from other sources. On July 5, 1902, Herzl recorded in his diary that he had a meeting with Lord Rothschild, a Jewish banking magnet, in which Herzl asked the Jewish financier to "prevent the Sultan from obtaining money"[33] from non-Zionist sources.

The Rothschilds had attained great power over international finance. Even half a century earlier, the Paris Rothschild could tell an agent of the American government who was in Europe trying to secure a loan for the United States Treasury: You may tell your government that you have seen the man who is at the head of the finances of Europe, and that he has told you that they cannot borrow a dollar not a dollar."[34] When the great financial power of the Rothschilds is considered, it becomes obvious that Herzl's method of "negotiating" with Turkey bordered unto blackmail.

---

[32] *Ibid.,* pp. 339-343.

[33] *Ibid.,* p. 367.

[34] Jenks, "British Capital," in Thomas C. Cochran and William Miller, *The Age of Enterprise.* (New York: Macmillan, 1924), p. 106.

In addition to the debt problem, the Turks were concerned about the deservedly bad press which they were receiving in Europe due to their brutal treatment of the Armenians at that time. The Turkish Sultan wanted to know if the Jews were willing to use the influence which he believed they had over the media of communications in order to muffle protest against Turkish persecution of the Armenians. Zionist writers had indignantly protested the suggestion that they, the victims of persecution, would accept to obtain their ends at the expense of other victims of persecution. They argued that "they were not so supine as to execute such a bargain [concerning the Armenian question] and reach their own goals over the dead bodies of another race."[35] The Zionists, however, did accept the bargain, the assertions of their publicists notwithstanding. The evidence that the Zionists were more "supine" than their publicists were willing to concede came from none other than their own prophet, Theodor Herzl. On May 3, 1896, Herzl recorded in his diary that Nevlinsky (an agent of the Turkish government) had asked Herzl to help him obtain the support of the Jews on the Armenian question, and Herzl "thought the idea was excellent" if the Sultan would render "a substantial counter-service to the Jewish cause."[36]

Five weeks later, Herzl repeated his assurances to Nevlinsky by saying: "Let the Sultan give us that parcel of land [Palestine], and in return we [the Jews] would set his

---

[35] Gottheil, *Zionism*, p. 94.
[36] Herzl, *Diaries*, p. 128.

house in order, regulate his finances, and influence world opinion in his favor."[37] On June 22, 1896, Herzl further confided to his diary:

> The service he [the Turkish Sultan] asks of me is this... I am to do what I can toward getting the European press (in London, Paris, Berlin, and Vienna) to deal with the Armenian question in a spirit more friendly to the Turks... I told Nevlinsky that I was ready *à me mettre en campagne.* Let them give me the facts I need on the Armenian situation: which persons in London to influence, what newspapers to win over, etc.[38]

Nor did the Zionist leader confine himself to promising Jewish support in suppressing the truth about the Armenian massacres, for he was prompt to act. On July 8, 1896, he recorded the following entry in his diary: "Yesterday I launched the Armenian business with Lucien Wolf. I asked him to start a little press-campaign for the purpose of calming public opinion on the Armenian question."[39]

Nevertheless, Herzl's efforts to have the Turkish Sultan cede Palestine to the Jews ended in failure. Nevlinsky, who was acting as an intermediary between the Zionists and the Turkish government, informed Herzl of the Sultans's refusal:

---

[37] *Ibid.,* p. 138.
[38] *Ibid.,* pp. 159-160.
[39] Herzl, *Diaries,* p. 176. Lucien Wolf was an English Jew who was at the time the foreign editor of the London *Daily Graphic,* and a contributor to other periodicals on foreign affairs.

I cannot sell even a foot of land [the Sultan was reported to have said], for it does not belong to me but to my people. They have won this Empire and fertilized it with their blood. We will cover it once more with our blood, before we allow it to be torn from us. Two of my regiments from Syria and Palestine allowed themselves to be killed to a man at Plevna. Not one of them yielded; one and all remained, dead, upon the field. The Turkish people own the Turkish Empire, not I. I can dispose of no part of it. The Jews may spare their millions. When my Empire is divided, perhaps they will get Palestine for nothing. But only our corpse can be divided.[40]

Whether the Sultan's words expressed his true motive for refusing to deliver Palestine to the Zionists is debatable. Nevertheless, his were prophetic words. Within less than 20 years, World War I had left Turkey a vanquished power, and the victorious Allies divided the spoils. Arab territory in Asia, with the exception of the Arabian Peninsula, was partitioned between France and Britain who proceeded to dispose of it in a manner compatible — or so they thought — with their imperial interests. Syria and Lebanon were to be France's share, and the British Empire was inflated further to include Iraq, Trans-Jordan, and Palestine.

---

[40] *Ibid.*, p. 152.

CHAPTER 3 - THE BALFOUR DECLARATION

While the Zionists organized and mobilized their forces for the purpose of converting their scheme into a reality, the Arab people were preoccupied with a struggle that was more urgent and, it seemed to them, more real than the Zionists' threat to Palestine. The struggle in which they were engaged at the time involved a clear and present threat to their national survival.

The Ottoman Empire in the latter part of the nineteenth century had degenerated into the most unenlightened despotism this side of the Dark Ages. The corrupt and tyrannical way in which it governed its territories in Europe is amply shown in history books, but it is less known that Arab territories under Ottoman rule fared no better. In addition to the usual forms of oppression, the Ottoman despots subjected the Arab people to what might be characterized as cultural genocide. Since the Arabs' language and cultural heritage have always been the backbone of their national consciousness, the Ottoman attempt to suppress that language, and by so doing to discourage the Arab people's awareness of their cultural achievements, was and was viewed by the Arab people as an attack upon their national identity.

The Arabs' endeavors to redress their grievances against their Ottoman rulers were similar to the American Colonies' efforts to redress their grievances against Britain. At first, they argued for more equitable representation in the government, and for a voice in their local affairs. It was not long, however, before the Arab people were made to realize that the Ottoman government was in no way inclined to grant autonomy to the subject peoples, and that it was determined to deal ruthlessly with any manifestations of national consciousness.

When World War I broke out, Turkey stood on the side of Germany. Britain was quite aware of Arab resentment against Turkish rule. It capitalized on this resentment by encouraging rebellion in order to tie up Turkish forces and facilitate the task of Britain, which was preparing to invade Turkish Middle Eastern possessions.

This mutual interest finally resulted in an agreement to the effect that the Arabs would rise in rebellion against Turkey, for which assistance to the allied cause Britain agreed to recognize Arab independence after the war. These agreements — contained in correspondence between McMahon, the British High Commissioner in Egypt, and Sharif Hussein of Mecca — have been a subject of dispute. The Zionists took the position that the British commitment to recognize Arab independence did not include Palestine. The Arab position is that Palestine was included. [41]

---

[41] For The Arab Point Of View See George Antonius, *The Arab Awakening* (New York: G. P. Putman's Sons, 1946). For a contrary

The Arabs took their commitment seriously and raised the banner of rebellion against Turkey in 1916. Britain, on the other hand, did not take its commitment as seriously. For while the Arabs fought on the side of the allies, Britain was secretly negotiating with Russia and France on the disposal of Arab lands then under Turkish rule. One result of the negotiations was the secret Sykes-Picot agreement between Britain and France. This agreement showed that Britain had no intention of honoring its commitment to the Arabs, and instead of recognizing their independence after the war, it was planning to partition their territories into British and French possessions.[42]

The cards were stacked against the Arab people. On one side of them stood the Ottoman Empire — the corrupt, oppressive conqueror they fought to overthrow. On the other side stood Britain and its allies who proclaimed sympathy for the Arabs' desire to be free, while they negotiated secretly to deny them that freedom.

In contrast, the Zionists were being courted practically on all sides. This courtship was to result in the Zionists attainment of the indispensable support for their cause which, until then, they had sought in vain. The endorsement of their scheme in relation to Palestine by

opinion see Paul L. Hanna, *British Policy in Palestine* (Washington, D.C.: American Council on Public Affairs, 1942).

[42] After the overthrow of the Czarist government in Russia, the Bolsheviks discovered papers pertaining to the secret negotiations and agreement and published them in *Izvestia* on November 24, 1917. Royal Institute of International Affairs, *Great Britain and Palestine, 1915-1945* (London: Oxford University Press, 1946) pp. 7-8.

one of the world's major powers was given by Britain in the form of the Balfour Declaration of 1917.[43]

The circumstances surrounding the birth of the Balfour Declaration offer a classic case study of how little justice matters when it clashes with the interests of an expansionist major power. It shows how, under such circumstances, a democratic country like Britain finds it possible to dismiss majority opinion and the right of self-determination as a mere "technical ingenuity."[44]

It shows how a strong-handed, indefensible transgression upon the rights of a defenseless people has been pictured as one of the most touching manifestations of humanitarianism ever to flow out of the kind heart of a great power. That type of distortion, which managed to effect such a miraculous transformation, has been employed so often and so effectively in connection with the Arab- Zionist dispute over Palestine that it is practically impossible to find a parallel to it.

It was said in the last chapter that after the establishment of the World Zionist Organization, Theodor Herzl attempted to induce Turkey to cede Palestine to the Zionists for the eventual establishment of a Jewish state. Britain and Germany made attempts to persuade the Ottoman government to grant the Zionists privileges

---

[43] This chapter is not intended to be a detailed narration of the history of the Balfour Declaration. For a detailed study of the Balfour Declaration see Leonard Stein's *The Balfour Declaration* (New York: Simon and Schuster, 1961).

[44] *Opinions and Arguments From Speeches and Addresses of the Earl Of Balfour* (Garden City: New York: Doubleday, Doran & Co., Inc., 1928) pp. 213-214.

which would further their designs upon Palestine. Herzl turned first to Germany for assistance as early as 1896. Germany was cultivating Turkey's friendship, an effort which succeeded in forging an alliance between the two countries when World War I loomed on the horizon. For this reason, Germany seemed to be the power best suited for the role of persuading Turkey to help the Zionist cause. The German government did intervene on behalf of the Jews and managed to be helpful in many ways: it "prevailed upon the Turks to refrain from a projected mass deportation of Jews of Russian nationality...helped to save a number of Jews occupying prominent positions in Palestine from imprisonment or expulsion,"[45] and it intervened with the Turks on many occasions at the request of the Constantinople Zionist office in matters affecting the Jewish minority in Palestine. It even went to the extent of allowing the Zionist Agency in Constantinople "to use the German diplomatic courier and telegraphic code for communicating with Berlin and Palestine."[46]

At that time, however, Germany saw fit to refrain from using the full weight of its influence on Turkey in its efforts to help the Zionists achieve their objective. It was restrained from doing so for several reasons: it was afraid of unduly offending the touchy Sultan who might think that Germany was arrogating for itself the position of protector of the Jews in Palestine just as the French had

---

[45] This much was conceded by Richard Lichtheim, who was in charge of the Zionist Agency in Constantinople at that time. Stein,*The Balfour Declaration*, p. 209.
[46] *Ibid.*, p. 210.

done in the Levant in relation to the Catholic population – a state of affairs which the Sultan considered to be a highly undesirable intervention in his empire's internal affairs. Germany also was fearful that its full patronage of the Zionist cause might get it entangled with the other powers which had or aspired to have a stake in Palestine. Moreover, it was discouraged by the fact that most influential German Jews were very much opposed to Zionism. Germany was also offended by the Jews in Palestine, who opposed the use of German as the language of instruction in their schools.[47]

The outcome of all this was that Germany practically lost interest in Zionism, until 1914 when the war and Germany's need for allies revived its interest in world Jewry. For the time being, however, the Zionists concluded that they must seek patronage from a power other than Germany.

Of all the remaining major powers which had or aspired to have an interest in the future of Palestine, Britain was the most likely candidate, and the Zionists concentrated their efforts in that country. The Zionists had already centered their economic and financial interests in Britain. In 1899, they had established there the Jewish Colonial Trust, which was to be the main financial instrument of the Zionist movement. In 1903, they incorporated the Anglo-Palestine Company. In 1907, the Jewish National Fund was established, followed by the Palestine Land Development Company in 1909. In addition to these assets, Britain offered other advantages

---

[47] *Ibid.*, pp. 21-22.

to the Zionist cause. It was a "free country" in which the Zionists could work for their cause without undue restraints, and where some Jews had attained high positions with considerable influence. For these and other reasons which will be pointed out shortly, "Theodor Herzl had from the start attached great importance to the British Jews. He had done everything in his power to interest them in his ideas about the nature of the Jewish problem and the way to deal with it, and had, in his own mind, cast them for a leading rôle in the execution of his plans."[48] Although such factors helped draw the Zionists to Britain in their search for a sponsoring power, they were not sufficiently powerful to lead to the consummation of an alliance between the Zionist Organization and the British government. The Zionists were realistic enough to know that they must find something appealing to British *interests* to bring about the partnership. This inducement was found in Britain's fear that some other power might get a firm foothold in Palestine — the little country with the great strategic position.

In those days it was even easier than now for a great power to impose itself upon a small country. It could, for example, claim that its presence there was essential to the security of its other possessions. Britain's interest in Egypt and the Suez Canal stemming from Britain's need for a convenient and a safe access to India may be said to typify this approach. Or it could proclaim itself as the guardian of a certain minority group in that country, and by so doing stake for itself a special position in it. This was done

---

[48] *Ibid.*, p. 17.

by France in relation to the Catholic population of the Levant. In its attempt to reserve for itself a privileged position in Palestine, Britain used both of these expedients. If Britain were to espouse Zionism and to become the protector of Jewish interests, it would be on an equal footing with Russia, the protector of the Orthodox, and with France, the protector of the Catholics.[49] In this way, Britain would make sure that it would not be at a disadvantage *vis-à-vis* other interested powers at the Peace Conference which was to decide the fate of the Middle East after the war.

Britain, as a matter of fact, began to prepare for its future role as the protector of Jewish interests in Palestine as far back as 1839, when Palestine was still under the actual control of Egypt and the nominal rule of Turkey. In that year Palmerston, who was Britain's foreign minister, instructed his diplomatic representatives in Palestine "to afford protection to the Jews generally," and in the following year he authorized Sir Moses Haim Montefiore, a prominent British Jew, "to write to the Jews of the East that if they had any serious complaints to make, the English Consuls would...forward them to the Ambassador in Constantinople" who would take up the matter with Turkish authorities there.[50] In 1841, he wrote to the British ambassador in Constantinople saying that the Jews should be encouraged to go to Palestine, and that "they should count on Britain for protection."[51]

---

[49] *Ibid.*, p. 8.
[50] *Ibid.*, p. 7.
[51] *Ibid.*

In order to persuade Turkey to be more favorably inclined toward the Zionist cause, the British government expressed the view that "the Jews...are... a sort of Freemason fraternity whose goodwill would be useful to the Sultan,"[52] and that "it is well known that the Jews of Europe possess great wealth, and it is manifest that any country in which a considerable number of them might choose to settle would derive great benefit from the riches which they would bring into it."[53]

The hypocrisy of this attitude becomes obvious when it is recalled that Britain was probably the first country to pass a law restricting Jewish immigration into its territory. But more on this later.

These early attempts on the part of Britain to persuade Turkey to favor Zionism met with no more success than similar attempts by Germany, and for reasons that were not entirely dissimilar. As in Germany, Jews in Britain were not very enthusiastic about the idea of "returning" to Palestine.

> The real force behind the movement for the restoration of the Jews to Palestine was 'the religious party'...a body of devout and high-minded English Christians who, looking at the ferment in the East, believed that the time was at hand for the fulfillment of prophecy by the return of the Chosen People to the Holy Land, and that it was God's will that the British

---

[52] *Ibid.*
[53] *Ibid.*, p. 6.

nation should be his instrument for achieving this purpose.[54]

If God was reluctant about keeping this commitment to the Jewish people, then the British nation should help the process along. It is interesting to note that a representative of this point of view was Lord Ashley (later the Seventh Earl of Shaftesbury), who belonged to the London Society for Promoting Christianity Among the Jews, and who believed that the idea that English Jews be eligible to sit in parliament was "an insult to Christianity."[55] This method of clothing the dictates of self- interest in the far more noble garb of humanitarianism and high ideals was to appear again and again in the handling of the problem of Palestine.

This initial British interest in Zionism waned and remained dormant until after the establishment of the Zionist organization toward the end of the century. Only this time Britain and Germany were heading toward conflict and their search for allies was assuming greater urgency. This search for allies proved to be the most advantageous thing that had happened to the Zionist cause up to that time.

The Zionists began to emphasize the strategic importance of Palestine, and to point out that Britain's best chance to secure it for itself was to help the Zionists establish themselves there. No power, the Zionists pointed out, "had the interest in Palestine that England had, seeing that England in Egypt was next-door neighbor

---

[54] *Ibid.*, p. 10.
[55] *Ibid.*, p. 11.

to Palestine and that the shortest way to India was through Palestine."[56]

Due to recent developments in weaponry and the crumbling of traditional imperial systems, Palestine has lost a great deal of its strategic significance. But at the time, Palestine's geographic location made it very important to Britain. An assessment of Palestine's position at that time found it to be "as important as Egypt from the point of view of British Imperial communications. Strategically, it is the eastern outpost against any potential threat to the Suez Canal; it is the outlet of the pipeline from Kirkuk; it is a halting place in the international air route to India and beyond, and it is a starting point for the desert motor road to Iraq"[57]

Britain, the Zionists knew, did not relish the possibility of seeing Palestine fall into the hands of another power. The Zionists proposed that this possibility could be forestalled if Britain would help them take over the country under British protection.[58] When the war broke out in 1914, the Zionists' chances of success improved immeasurably.

Not long after World War I began, it developed into a war of attrition, and it was apparent that neither side was to gain a speedy victory. By 1916 it had degenerated into a senseless slaughter, and the adversaries faced each

---

[56] *Ibid.*, p. 19.

[57] Royal Institute of International Affairs, *Great Britain and Palestine, 1915-1945* p. 1.

[58] Dr. Haim Weizman, who later became Israel's first president. Quoted in Blanche E. C. Dugdale, *Arthur James Balfour* (New York: G. P. Putnam's Sons, 1937), vol. 2, p. 164.

other across a ribbon of fire and hate and rotten human flesh. And it seemed as if the insanity were destined to endure forever.

If the slaughter was to cease, something had to happen to tip the even scales, and each side naturally wanted them to tip in its favor. Next to Providential intervention, America's entry into the war was the factor most likely to decide the outcome of the struggle. Both parties to the struggle knew this, and both of them bent their efforts to influence America's attitude toward the war. For this purpose, both Germany and Britain counted heavily on the great influence which they believed the Jews to have in many countries, and especially in the United States.

The idea that Jewish influence in the United States "was potent in the formulation of public sentiment"[59] was very likely exaggerated. It is true that their influence was far from negligible, but it is also doubtful that it was potent enough to sway the United States one way or the other in its attitude toward World War I. The important thing, however, is not whether or not world Jewry possessed the great influence attributed to them, but the fact that *they were believed to possess it*.

There is no question that both Germany and Britain believed Jewish influence to be sufficiently powerful to make it worth appeasing. In their efforts to persuade Turkey to adopt a more favorable attitude towards Zionism, both Germany and Britain pointed out the advantages which would presumably accrue to Turkey by

---

[59] Hanna, British Policy in Palestine, p. 36.

befriending powerful world Jewry. Knowing that the Jews "might well be influenced in either direction by what happened in Palestine,"[60] they began to compete in their support of Zionism.

In November 1915, Germany informed its consuls in Turkey that it looked favorably on "Jewish activities designed to promote the economic and cultural progress of the Jews in Turkey, and also on the immigration and settlement of Jews from other countries."[61] Also, the German press began to allude to the possibility of a Jewish state in Palestine.[62] The Zionists, of course, prodded Germany to make more definite commitments on behalf of their cause by pointing out that "Germany would be well-advised, in her own interests, to cooperate with the Zionists...[who] could be relied upon to spread German culture, and promote German economic penetration, throughout the Turkish empire."[63]

Britain's belief that world Jews were a power to reckon with was apparent throughout its dealings with Zionists. This idea that "in spite of appearances, the Jews were a force in the world and could be useful friends...was to reappear again and again in the British handling of the Palestine question in 1916-1917."[64] Just as Germany's need for allies and its belief that the Jews' friendship would benefit its cause led to a revival of its interest in Zionism, similar needs and beliefs on the part of Britain

---

[60] Stein, p. 208.
[61] *Ibid.*, pp. 213-214.
[62] Dugdale, v. 2, p. 166.
[63] Stein, pp. 212-213.
[64] *Ibid.*, p. 6.

resulted in a renewed effort to bring about a British-Zionist alliance.

Negotiations between the two parties finally brought about an understanding, and on November 2, 1917, Britain gave the Zionists the great power sponsorship which they needed to implement their planned take-over of Palestine. This British commitment took the form of a letter addressed to Lord Rothschild, President of the British Zionist Foundation. The letter, whose second paragraph came to be known as the Balfour Declaration (after the name of the British Foreign Secretary, its author), ran as follows:

Foreign Office,

November 2nd, 1917.

Dear Lord Rothschild,

I have much pleasure in conveying to you, on behalf of His Majesty's Government, the following declaration of sympathy with Jewish Zionist aspirations which has been submitted to, and approved by, the Cabinet.

His Majesty's Government view with favour the establishment in Palestine of a national home for the Jewish people, and will use their best endeavours to facilitate the achievement of this object, it being clearly understood that nothing shall be done which may prejudice the civil and religious rights of existing non-Jewish communities in Palestine, or the rights and political status enjoyed by Jews in any other country.

I should be grateful if you would bring this declaration to the knowledge of the Zionist Federation.[65]

Events had shown that Theodor Herzl was quite right when, in 1903, he said that the Zionists would get Palestine "not from the good will but from the jealousy of the Powers."[66]

Years later, when the Palestine problem was being discussed in the United Nations and elsewhere, the Zionists used the Balfour declaration as the cornerstone of their case. The Arabs of Palestine, who constituted more than ninety percent of the country's population when the Balfour declaration was issued, have consistently maintained that it was made against the wishes of the preponderant majority of the people and that the declaration was, therefore, invalid. They further stated that the Balfour declaration was in violation of previous Arab-British agreements as these were contained in the McMahon correspondence by which Britain had pledged itself to recognize Arab independence for their revolt against Turkey during the war. The Balfour declaration was also held to be in violation of the Allied war aims as these were stated in President Wilson's Fourteen Points, because it denied to the Arabs of Palestine the right of self-determination.

A great many words have been uttered in the course of debate over the question of what the Balfour declaration actually meant. It serves no purpose to repeat

---

[65] *Ibid.*, p. ii.
[66] *Ibid.*, p. 25.

or to elaborate on these arguments here. One can even reasonably argue that the Balfour declaration meant nothing or more accurately perhaps, different things to different people. Musing over this aspect of the conflict (if "musing" can be properly used in connection with anything related to Palestine's tragedy), a British author once said: "It is futile to quibble over the wording of the Balfour declaration as it is to quibble over the wording of the McMahon, correspondence. The wording of both is vague and ambiguous because it was intended to be vague and ambiguous." "Balfour," this same writer continued, "was a typical Conservative politician, a man to whom equivocation was a mere matter of routine."[67]

Equivocation might have been a "mere matter of routine" with Lord Balfour and with his Conservative fellow politicians, but the ambiguity of the Balfour declaration was more than the product of mere habit. The British government was aiming for the avoidance of a clear commitment in Palestine which might hamper its own plans for the Near East. India was the dazzling jewel in the crown of Imperial Britain, the Suez Canal was the route to India, and Palestine was the eastern flank of the Suez Canal. Britain had plans for Palestine.

Although Lord Balfour, in a speech to the Zionist Federation on July 12, 1920, said: "For long I have been a convinced Zionist,"[68] actually he "knew very little about Zionism and absolutely nothing about the Near East and

---

[67] John Marlowe, *Rebellion in Palestine.* (London: The Cresset Press, 1946), p. 41.
[68] *Opinions and Arguments*, p. 211.

had neither the time nor the inclination to learn about either. What was wanted was a formula which would enable Great Britain, with the assent of the Allied Powers, to establish herself in Palestine after the war."[69] Britain, true to her diplomatic tradition, rose to the occasion and the wanted formula was found. Lloyd George, who was Britain's Prime Minister at the time, didn't "care a damn for the Jews or their past or their future,"[70] but he thought that the Zionist movement could be used as a "wooden horse of Troy to introduce British control into Palestine. The British government came to view it in that light. If the Jews were to be established in Palestine, the British would be their natural 'protectors'... And so the British Government adopted Zionism."[71]

The Zionists, it must be pointed out, were not averse to allowing their movement to be used as the "wooden horse of Troy" if by so doing they improved their chances of attaining their goals. In his *Diaries*, Theodor Herzl had made it abundantly clear that he had given several major powers, including Germany and Britain, to understand that if they would take the Zionist movement under their protective wings, they would have, in a Jewish state in Palestine, a base of operations in the heart of the Arab

---

[69] Marlowe, p. 40. It is possible, however, that Balfour was bothered by a feeling of guilt due to Jewish persecution in Christian countries. His niece had written: "I remember in childhood imbibing from him [Balfour] the idea that Christian religion and civilization owes to Judaism an immeasurable debt, shamefully ill repaid." Dougdale, v. 2, p. 324.

[70] Remark by Lord Asquith quoted in Antonius, *The Arab Awakening,* p. 264.

[71] Marlowe, pp. 39-40.

world. This fact moved one writer to "discount the importance of Jewish immigration as a factor in Arab objection to the Balfour declaration and to conclude that it was the fact that the Jews were the stool pigeons of British Imperialism that damned the whole business in Arab eyes from the beginning."[72]

It seems to be impossible to mention the Balfour declaration without relating the myth of the acetone. This myth has it that the British government pledged itself to facilitate the establishment of a Jewish "national home" in Palestine as some token of appreciation to Haim Weizmann, a British chemist who had discovered during the war a process for making acetone, a substance used in the manufacture of high explosives.

The question of what motivates people to do the things they do is always a difficult one to answer with certainty, but to suppose that the British government goes around rewarding its scientists with countries is surely too simple an explanation of British foreign politics. It is more plausible, to put it mildly, that Weizmann's chemical formula was helpful in establishing better contacts between the Zionists and British officials, which facilitated British Zionist negotiations, which ultimately led to issuing the Balfour declaration.

The motives, however, behind the British Zionist alliance which led to the Balfour declaration, were purely self-interest. As it was stated previously, these motives were the desire of the British government to induce world Jewry to use whatever influence they had over the hatch-

---

[72] *Ibid.*, p. 46.

eries of public opinion—the media of communications—
in favor of the Allies during the war, and to establish
British control in Palestine.

CHAPTER 4 - THE MANDATE

It was stated previously that in order to give their creed a more favorable public image, the Zionists clothed what was essentially a political ambition of a minority group with a maze of myths which made it appear as the undying and almost mystical attachment to an ancient home to which they wished to "return." In order to gain for their aims the sympathy and the support of the world, the Zionists did not confine themselves to making the nature of their movement appear to be what it was not, but they also managed to advertise their endeavors to attain sovereignty over Palestine in such a way as to create the sympathy-evoking impression that they were fulfilling their aims against incredible odds.

To achieve this objective, Zionist writers and publicists — at the expense of historical accuracy — interpreted the period of British mandate over Palestine in such a way as to make it conform to the desired image. The result of this endeavor was a distorted picture of the situation which afflicted Palestine when, in 1947, The United Nations was called upon to deal with the problem.

The standard Zionist interpretation ran as follows: the British government pledged itself, in the Balfour declaration, to use its "best endeavours" to facilitate the establishment of a Jewish "national home" in Palestine. The Allies and associated powers subsequently issued similar statements which meant that they, too, favored such a scheme. The Supreme Allied (San Remo) Conference of 1920 entrusted the government of Palestine to Great Britain so it could carry out its pledge to the Jewish people. In 1922, the League of Nations made Britain responsible for placing the country under such political, administrative, and economic conditions as would secure the establishment of a Jewish national home. Contrary to its pledges, Britain used its mandate for Palestine to obstruct the establishment of the national home instead of facilitating it as it was pledged to do. In asking for the creation of a Jewish state in Palestine, as they did when the United Nations became seized of the question in 1947, the Zionists were merely upholding the international agreements which Britain was evidently unwilling to honor. Thus ran the Zionist argument.

There are three things wrong with this interpretation of the mandate. First, it takes the validity of the Balfour declaration for granted. It was said in the previous chapter that the compatibility of the declaration with *prior* British commitments to the Arabs was, at best questionable. More important, the declaration was merely a unilateral statement by the British government issued during the war to further British war and imperial objectives when Britain was not yet in control of the country, let alone possessing a right to dispose of it contrary to the wishes of its people.

The most interested party, the Arab people of Palestine, not only refused to acquiesce in Britain's agreement with the non-Palestinian Zionists, but they also manifested their objection to it expressly and persistently.

Mr. Bevin once called this unilateral character of the Balfour declaration it's "tragedy," because "neither its British authors nor its American and British supporters had taken account of the Arabs."[73]

Whether or not Britain could subordinate the wishes and interests of the people of Palestine to its imperial objectives is not the point. The point is whether or not such action could have the legitimacy of a binding international agreement or a validity which the people of Palestine could be called upon to recognize. This legitimacy or validity could be admitted only if it were conceded that might makes right. It is assumed here that there exists a consensus among civilized peoples that might does not make right, although it may make *possible*. By basing their claims upon Palestine on the Balfour declaration, therefore, the Zionists were relying upon the backing of superior force while they were erroneously equating that backing with international law.

It is interesting to note that the Balfour declaration did not confine itself to recognizing and supporting "Jewish Zionist aspirations" in relation to Palestine. It also was supposed to protect "the rights and political status enjoyed by the Jews in any other country."[74] It is a matter of common knowledge that since the Balfour declaration was issued on November 2, 1917, "the rights and political status enjoyed by the Jews," like those enjoyed by other minority groups, have been violated or restricted in many countries and on different occasions. If the Balfour

[73] Royal Institute of International Affairs, *Ibid.*, p. 143.
[74] The text of the Balfour Declaration was quoted in Chapter 2.

declaration were seriously considered to be a binding international agreement (as the Zionist and their supporters claimed that it was), why was it not invoked in defense of those rights? Why is it considered to be international law in relation to Palestine while in relation to other countries it was not considered to have any validity or applicability? The Balfour declaration was an instrument of British policy, not an instrument of law. The claim that the declaration was an instrument of international law which any nation could be called upon to respect was nothing more than an attempt to sanctify a statement of British foreign policy which favored Zionist objectives.

The second aspect of the Zionist interpretation which gives it a distorting effect is the unjustifiable assumption that by promising to assist in the establishment of a Jewish "national home" in Palestine, Britain was pledged to help establish a Jewish state based on a Jewish majority. The fact of the matter was that the British government itself was not sure of what it had actually promised to do in Palestine. The numerous reports, white papers, and policy statements on Palestine issued by the government during its mandate shows Britain's uncertainty about what it was "supposed" to do with the country. For example, a comparison of the 1922 (Churchill) White Paper with the 1939 White Paper clearly shows the absence of any definite concept on the part of Britain regarding the precise meaning and the scope of its commitments in Palestine. The only thing which the British government seems to have had in mind with sufficient clarity was to assure British control over the country. The nursing of a Jewish "national home" was not the *reason* but the *means* of securing that control from the Allies. Britain could point to the Balfour declaration and with an expression of piety proclaim: "we have pledged ourselves to help the long-persecuted Jewish people to have a home of their own in Palestine. We need to be there in order to be able to do so."

Britain obtained its Mandate from the San Remo Conference in 1920, and its presence in Palestine was granted. What it needed after getting into the country was a justification for staying there until its interests allowed it to move out. The Arab-Jewish conflict of which the Zionist ambition was the seed, provided such a "justification." Britain had a pretext for making the claim that its presence in Palestine was needed for the maintenance of law and order. Other than the object of being in Palestine, Britain had none. It was not yet ready to see an independent Palestine (neither Arab nor Jewish nor both) from which it would have had to clear out.

In 1947, India became independent. Egypt was on its way to regaining complete sovereignty and, consequently, Palestine—the eastern flank of the Suez Canal—was losing its strategic value as a post along the lines of British imperial communications. When that time arrived, Britain could afford to look with more benevolence upon the prospect of seeing itself dislodged from Palestine. It was not a coincidence that it was not until 1947 that Britain admitted the unworkability of its mandate and "restored" to the United Nations the authority to dispose of the Holy Land.

It can be seen, then, that to assert, as the Zionists did, that the purpose of British presence in Palestine was to establish a Jewish state based on a Jewish majority was to give the Balfour declaration a meaning which even Britain was not sure that it had. Moreover, such an assertion gave the problem of Palestine an accent which in reality it lacked. It served to make it appear to be a quarrel between Britain and Palestine's Jewish minority with the Arab majority being merely a subsidiary complication dimly visible in the background. The Zionists had managed to be so much more vociferous than the Palestinian Arabs that public opinion in many countries did actually view the problem of Palestine as a dispute between Britain and the Jews with the Arabs somehow being there too. Such a view which relegated the majority of the people of Palestine to the peripheral position of "being there too" obviously is not conducive to a clear understanding of the situation.

The third way in which the Zionist interpretation of the British Mandate for Palestine contributed to confusing the nature of the problem was the fact that they put the emphasis on the wrong syllable. This distortion was accomplished by representing the Palestine problem as a *result* of what Britain failed to do for the Zionists while it was largely the outcome of what Britain had actually *done* for them. The rest of this chapter will be devoted to a discussion of this point.

* * *

When the World Zionist Organization was established in 1897 to seek the implementation of the idea of a Jewish state, Palestine became a *potential* source of

45

Arab-Jewish conflict. When the British government issued the Balfour Declaration in which it expressed its sympathy with Zionist aims and its intention to assist in their realization, the conflict became *actual*.

Herzl and his Zionist Organization could write all the pamphlets they wanted, hold as many conferences as they had time for, and collect all the funds they could keep track of, but without being in Palestine in sufficient numbers, and without having the government of Palestine in the hands of a power sympathetic to their aspirations, the Zionists could not wrest Palestine from the hands of its Arab inhabitants. The Balfour Declaration was the password which gave the Zionists the means of imposing their presence upon the people of Palestine with the sanction of a great power.

The importance of having their aims recognized and sponsored by a major power was so clearly understood by the Zionists that they would not even begin to implement their scheme without such support. Theodor Herzl, the first president of the World Zionist Organization and whose brand of Zionism dominated the movement, had actually opposed further Jewish immigration to Palestine until great power endorsement of Zionism was secured. His diaries testify to the extent of his efforts to convince the wealthy Jews of Europe that it was futile and a waste of time and money to go on supporting and increasing Jewish settlements in Palestine in the absence of a great power guarantee of the Zionist program. Herzl correctly believed that the whole idea of a Jewish state would be a mere "romance" without great power support.[75]

By giving the Zionists the great power endorsement which they needed (in the form of the Balfour declaration), Britain kept the Zionist scheme from remaining a mere "romance" and, consequently, the potential Arab-Jewish conflict over Palestine became actual. Without the Balfour Declaration (or its equivalent) Zionism was no more than an impertinence in the eyes of the Palestinian Arabs. With the Declaration, Zionism became a threat to their homeland, and they became hostile to further Jewish immigration and understandably resentful toward the Jewish minority already living within the country. This, then, was the first major contribution of the British government toward the creation of a hitherto nonexistent Arab-Jewish conflict.

The second major contribution of the British Mandate to Palestine's tragedy was the persistent denial to the Arab people of Palestine of the right to govern their own country. It must be pointed out at the outset that Britain's denial of independence to Palestine at the end of the First World War and thereafter was not motivated by a belief in the unfitness of its people for self-government. The Covenant of the League of Nations had classified all the Mandated Arab territories (Syria, Lebanon, Palestine, Trans-Jordan, and Iraq) which were "liberated" from Turkey as "A" mandates. This meant that these territories "have reached a stage of development where their

---

[75] Herzl, who was seeking German recognition and support of Zionism, wrote: "If I do not convince Bismarck, or if he even declines to see me—well, the whole thing was a romance." Herzl, *Diaries*, p. 53.

existence as independent nations can be provisionally recognized subject to the rendering of *administrative advice and assistance.*"[76]

The Covenant further stated that "the wishes of these communities must be a principal consideration in the selection of the Mandatory Power" which was to render such administrative advice and assistance.[77] Not only had the Mandatory Powers (Britain and France) ruled mandated Arab territories as colonies, but the selection of the Mandatory Powers was not based upon the wishes of the communities concerned.

The selection of a Mandatory Power for Palestine was made by the "Principal Allied Powers." This fact is stated without equivocation in the League of Nations document relating to the Mandate for Palestine. In its preamble the document states: "Whereas the Principal Allied Powers have agreed, for the purpose of giving effect to the provisions of Article 22 of the Covenant of the League of Nations, to entrust to a *Mandatory selected by the said Powers* the administration of the territory of Palestine..."[78]

This document, which was intended to put Article 22 of the covenant into effect, was not in accord with that Article. Whereas Article 22 stipulated that the wishes of the people must be "a principal consideration in the

---

[76] League of Nations, *Covenant*, Article 22, paragraph 4.
[77] *Ibid.*
[78] League of Nations Document, C. 529. M. 314. 1922. VI. The document is reproduced in Llewellyn Pfankuchen, *A Documentary Textbook in International Law.* (New York: Rinehart & Company, Inc., 1940) pp. 76-83. (Italics added).

selection of the Mandatory," the document on the mandate for Palestine stated blandly that the choice of the mandatory was made by the principal allied powers and it did not as much as mention the wishes of the people concerned.

Not only was article 22 violated by the Principal Allied Powers who failed to ascertain the wishes of the people of Palestine, but they also acted *contrary* to these people's wishes.

The Syrian people knew that their country's fate was to be determined by the Peace Conference of the victorious powers at the end of the war. They also knew that the Allied powers were pledged to base their decision on the wishes of the people concerned. A General Syrian Congress was convened in 1919 in Damascus in order to formulate and to express the wishes of the people regarding the future government of Syria, which then included Palestine. The delegates were duly chosen representatives of the Syrian people, and their *Resolutions*[79] represented an unequivocal statement of their wishes. What the Syrian people wanted was, among other things, the independence of Syria and the preservation of its unity.

That the *Resolutions* of the Congress were truly representative of the popular will was confirmed by the King-Crane Commission, which was sent to Syria by President Wilson for the specific purpose of ascertaining the wishes of the Syrian people. The Commission reported

---

[79] A translation of the *Resolutions* is found in Antonius, *The Arab Awakening*. Appendix.

that the overwhelming majority of the people stated their opposition to having France as a Mandatory Power in any part of Syria, and that only a small minority gave first preference to Britain having such a mandate. Their first choice was the independence of their country or, if it had to be placed under the mandate of one of the powers, they wanted that power to be the United States. The King-Crane Commission put it this way:

> Our survey left no room for doubt of the choice of the majority of the Syrian people. Although it was not known whether America would take a Mandate at all; and although the Commission could not only give no assurances upon that point, but had rather to discourage expectations; nevertheless, upon the face of the returns, America was the first choice of 1,152 of the petitions presented—more than sixty percent for first choice.

> And the conferences showed that the people knew the grounds upon which they registered their choice for America. They declared that their choice was due to knowledge of America's record; the unselfish aims with which she had come into the War; the faith in her felt by multitudes of Syrians who had been in America; the spirit revealed in American educational institutions in Syria...their belief that America had no territorial or colonial ambitions, and would willingly withdraw when the Syrian State was well established as her treatment of both Cuba and the Philippines

seemed to them to illustrate; her genuinely democratic spirit; and her ample resources.[80]

In other words, the Mandate over Syria was given to the two powers which were specifically rejected by the people of the country. This act, coupled with the fact that the opposition of the people of Palestine to the Balfour Declaration was ignored by the Allied Powers added up to the most serious violation by the Allies of their own pledges so solemnly given during the war. The King-Crane Commission summed this aspect of the question as follows:

> In his address of July 4, 1918, President Wilson laid down the following principle as one of the four great "ends for which the associated peoples of the world were fighting": "The settlement of every question, whether of territory, of sovereignty, of economic arrangement, or of political relationship upon the basis of the free acceptance of that settlement by the people immediately concerned, and not upon the basis of the material interest or advantage of any other nation or people which may desire a different settlement for the sake of its own exterior influence or mastery." If that principle is to rule, and so the wishes of Palestine's population are to be decisive as to what is to be done with Palestine, then it is to be remembered that the non-Jewish population of Palestine—nearly nine-tenths of the whole—are emphatically against the entire Zionist

---

[80] *Ibid.*, Appendix.

programme. The tables show that there was no one thing upon which the population of Palestine were more agreed upon than this. To subject a people so minded to unlimited Jewish immigration, and to steady financial and social pressure to surrender the land, would be a gross violation of the principle just quoted, and of the people's rights, though it kept within the forms of law.[81]

In spite of this clear statement of popular will, Syria was partitioned, with one part of the country (present day Syria and Lebanon) placed under the mandate of France, and Britain was granted mandatory power over the rest of the country (Palestine and Trans-Jordan). The post war dismemberment of Syria and the withholding of self-government from its people were indispensable steps toward the fulfillment of the Zionist plan of establishing a Jewish state in Palestine. If Palestine had been given its independence after the First World War, or if it had been allowed to be a part of a larger independent Arab state as its people desired, the Palestine tragedy would not have come to pass. Without the Zionist threat to Palestine which the British Mandate was making clear and present, there was nothing inevitable about an Arab-Jewish conflict.

The third aspect of British administration which ultimately led to bloodshed and to the present-day Arab-Israeli stalemate was its immigration policy and its

[81] *Ibid.*, Appendix.

consequences. At the end of the First World War, the population of Palestine was estimated to be 650,000. A little over ninety percent were Arabs, and a little under ten percent were Jews.[82] Within the less than thirty years which intervened between the end of the First World War and the termination of the British Mandate in 1948, the Arab population of Palestine had doubled (from 600,000 to 1,200,000). The Jewish population, on the other hand, had increased eleven times during the same period. It had risen from about 55,000 to 600,000. The increase in the Arab population was almost entirely due to natural growth.[83] In contrast, the increase in the Jewish population was almost entirely due to immigration from foreign countries. In other words, although the Arab birth rate was higher than the Jewish birth rate in Palestine, the Jewish population of the country was increasing, on the average, five and a half times faster than the Arab population. The Arab people of Palestine were obviously justified in their fear that British administration of Palestine was reducing the Arab majority to a minority status and transforming the Jewish minority into a majority. In the meantime, Zionist and pro-Zionist press all over the world was waging a campaign the purpose of which was to put further pressure on the British

---

[82] the population and immigration figures used in this chapter are taken mainly from the Palestine Department of Immigration Reports cited in the Royal Institute of International Affairs' study quoted previously.

[83] in 1938, which was a "peak-year" of Arab immigration into Palestine, only 473 Arabs were permitted to enter the country as immigrants.

government to open Palestine to unlimited Jewish immigration.

Illegal Jewish immigration, which was assuming considerable proportions in the 1930s,[84] was defended as being necessary in the face of the "restrictive" immigration policy of the Mandatory Power.[85] This was accompanied by a growing pressure on the mandatory power from foreign governments which asked that unlimited Jewish immigration into Palestine be permitted. The policy of the Palestine government was to allow Jewish immigration up to the economic absorptive capacity of the country, as the *Annual Report* of the Administration of Palestine, 1933, had pointed out. To ask of Palestine — a country of slightly more than 10,000 square miles of territory — to shoulder the burden of serving as a haven for an unlimited number of people was

---

[84] One estimate puts the volume of illegal immigration after 1931 as "20% of the total legal immigration." (Marlowe, p. 130.) Palestine government official estimate gives the figure 22,400 for illegal immigration in the years 1932 and 1933, compared to 39,880 recorded immigrants. In 1939, 16,405 legal and 12,442 illegal Jewish immigrants entered Palestine. (Government figures cited in Royal Institute of International Affairs, *Ibid.*, pp. 63-64.)

[85] the fact, which is often conveniently ignored by the Zionists and the advocates of their cause, is that in some years not enough Jews could be found who wished to immigrate to Palestine to fill the legal quota. From 13,081 in 1926, Jewish immigration fell to 2,178 in 1928. In these particular years, the slackening of immigration was caused, not by restrictive policies, but "mainly by a fall in the exchange value of the Polish zloty. This made it impossible for Jews to leave Poland without exercising heavy losses in realizing their possessions, and thus put a virtual stop for the time to immigration from Poland, a country with the largest Jewish population in Europe." (Marlowe, p.121.)

patently unreasonable. And yet, when the Passfield Commission in its White Paper of 1930 that the mandatory government could restrict or, if necessary, suspend immigration to combat unemployment, the recommendation was attacked as "whittling down" the Mandate.[86]

It seems that the only possible explanations for such demands would be that the countries which wanted Palestine opened to "unrestricted" Jewish immigration were either grossly uninformed about conditions there, or that they were themselves unwilling to admit Jews into their own territories. In 1944, both American major political parties in the presidential campaign of that year included provisions in their platforms favoring the opening of Palestine to unlimited Jewish immigration. The Republican Party's platform stated:

In order to give refuge to millions of distressed Jewish men, women, and children driven from their homes by tyranny, we call for the opening of Palestine to their unrestricted immigration and land ownership, so that in accordance with the full intent and purpose of the Balfour Declaration of 1917 and the resolution of a Republican Congress in 1922, Palestine may be constituted as a free and democratic commonwealth. We condemn the failure of the President to insist that the mandatory of Palestine carry out the provision of the Balfour

[86] Bernard Joseph, *British Rule in Palestine.* (Washington, D.C., Public Affairs Press, 1948), p. 132.

55

Declaration and of the Mandate while he pretends to support them.[87]

The Democratic Party's platform said: "We favor the opening of Palestine to unrestricted Jewish immigration and colonization, and such a policy as to result in the establishment there of a free and democratic Jewish commonwealth."[88] Not to be outdone, President Roosevelt sent with (Senator) Robert Wagner a message to the annual convention of the Zionist Organization in America, which was conveniently meeting just before the presidential elections (October, 1944), in which he said about his party's views on Palestine quoted above: "... if reelected I shall help to bring about its realization."[89]

The hypocrisy of such pronouncements becomes evident when one contrasts them and many others like them made by American politicians and responsible public officials with the fact that several attempts were made at the time to reach a solution to the displaced persons' problem, and that "all these efforts had come to nothing, *primarily* because the restrictive [American] legislation of the past prevented American negotiators from making any commitments on behalf of their government."[90] The American authorities not only did not open their country's doors a little wider, but also administered their country's existing immigration laws in

---

[87] V. O. Key, *Politics, Parties, and Pressure Groups*. (New York: Thomas Y. Crowell Co., 1948), p. 741.

[88] *Ibid.*, p. 730.

[89] Joseph, p. 168.

[90] Oscar Handlin, *The American People in the Twentieth Century*. (Cambridge: Harvard University Press, 1954), p. 210. (Italics added).

a restrictive manner. In the period 1933 to 1944, during which the need for asylum was particularly great, the "American [immigration] quota had been so administered as to cut down the number of immigrants to 16.8 [percent] of the quota."[91] the result was that in this decade of greatest need for leniency in admitting aliens we find "the lowest immigration figures for a hundred years."[92]

If both American major political parties were so concerned about the fate of the displaced persons, they could have modified their "previous legislation" for the purpose of admitting them, or a sufficient number of them, into the United states to alleviate the problem. Their total control of the legislative and executive branches of the federal government would have made this an easy task. Obviously, they were not interested in doing so. Nor was Britain, another country which professed a great concern about the suffering of the Jewish people. Britain even went so far as to pass legislation specifically designed to keep them out of its territory. After the turn of the century, Jewish refugees began arriving in England in large numbers from Eastern Europe. Alluding to these events, Chamberlain addressed a British audience on December 15, 1904, by saying:

> You are suffering from the unrestricted import of cheaper goods. You are suffering also from the unrestricted immigration of the people who make these goods... The best solution of this question was to find some country in this

---

[91] Ibid.

[92] Richard Crossman, Palestine Mission: A Personal Record (New York: Harper and Brothers, 1947), p. 46.

57

world of ours... Some place in which these poor exiles...could dwell in safety...and where they could find subsistence without in any way infringing with the subsistence of others.[93]

Of course, British government objections to Jewish immigration were not limited to speech making. A bill restricting immigration was introduced by the Balfour government (ironically enough) and became a law in 1905.[94] this act prompted *The Jewish Chronicle* of May 5, 1905, to invite "Balfour to explain how his sympathy with persecuted Jews could be reconciled with a policy which led him 'to refuse asylum to Jewish religious refugees.'"[95]

Germany had a similar attitude, and the reference is not to Nazi Germany but to Imperial Germany which also expressed sympathy for the Zionist cause. "There are among your people," the Kaiser confided to Herzl, "certain elements whom it would be a good thing to move to Palestine."[96]

So neither the United States nor Britain nor Germany were willing to open their doors to more than a trickle of Jewish refugees. "Nor was any other country eager to open its door to such newcomers."[97] Instead, all the powers seemed to be determined to be humanitarian at the expense of the Arab people of Palestine, the people who were the least able to afford the luxury of being generous. Their little country was already becoming

---

[93] Quoted from *The Times*, December 16, 1904, by Stein, p. 33.
[94] Stein, p. 32 and p. 79.
[95] *Ibid.*, p. 150.
[96] Herzl, *The Jewish State*, p. 45.
[97] Handlin, p. 193.

overcrowded, especially when the high birth rate of the Palestinian Arabs is taken into consideration, as it must be. The density of population was about 180 persons per square mile in Palestine and less than 50 persons in the United States. Palestine was one of the most densely populated countries on earth, but it was pictured as a sparsely populated land where an unlimited number of Jews could still go and settle without infringing upon the rights of the country's inhabitants. The absurdity of this contention becomes manifest when one reflects upon the fact that the United States would have to have at least 450 million people living within its present borders before it could become as densely populated as Palestine was at the end of the Second World War.[98]

A study of Palestine population figures would have made clear the fact that the establishment of a Jewish state based on a Jewish majority could be accomplished only by the forceful eviction of the majority of its people, as actually happened in 1948 when the state of Israel was established.

Zionist propaganda before partition led to many people the world over to believe that Palestine was a sparsely inhabited country, and it was not until our refugees began pouring out of the country that people began to wonder where all these refugees were coming from. Indications that the establishment of a Jewish state in Palestine would result in a grave injustice to its Arab population were not lacking. As early as 1919, the King-

---

[98] Editors Note: The U.S. population was less than 147 million in 1948.

Crane Commission, which visited the area at the behest of President Wilson, and whose members admitted that they "began their study of Zionism with minds predisposed in its favor,"[99] reported that its observations and conferences with Jewish representatives had convinced it of the fact that the establishment of a Jewish state could not be accomplished "without the gravest trespass upon the civil and religious rights of existing non-Jewish [Muslim and Christian] communities in Palestine,"[100] rights which the Balfour Declaration was also supposed to protect. A scientist sympathizer conceded that "before the nineteen twenties were over, no fair-minded person could deny that in the process of building the Jewish state a grave injustice would be done to the Arabs."[101]

Testifying before the Anglo- American Committee of Inquiry on Palestine, which was set up in 1946 to study the problem, Dr. Frank W. Notestein, director of the Office of Population Research at Princeton University, said that "in view of the high Arab birth rate and the decline in the Arab death rate... a permanent Jewish majority in Palestine could not be maintained unless some of the Arabs were *moved out*, because the Arabs increased twice as fast as the Jews."[102]

---

[99] From King-Crane Commission Reported reproduced in Antonius, pp. 443-458.

[100] *Ibid*.

[101] Richard H. S. Crossman, *A Nation Rebord* (New York: Atheneum Publishers, 1960), p. 61.

[102] Bartley C. Crum, *Behind the Silken Curtain*. (New York: Simon and Schuster, 1947), pp. 22-23. (Italics added.)

The realization that the establishment of a Jewish state in Palestine was not possible without infringing upon the historic rights of the Palestinian Arabs was reflected in a resolution of the British Labour Party Conference of December, 1944, which called for a policy which would "let the Jews if they wish enter this tiny land [Palestine] in such numbers as to become a majority...the Arabs being encouraged to move out as the Jews moved in."[103]

In a speech before the British House of Commons on November 13, 1945, Mr. Bevin, then foreign secretary, stated that "the problem created by Nazi aggression was not one which could be dealt with only in relation to Palestine; it would need a united effort by the Powers to relieve the miseries of these suffering peoples."[104] Nevertheless, this "united effort by the Powers" failed to materialize. The Powers had, instead, sought to placate their consciences, not by doing something themselves, but by insisting that the Arabs of Palestine pay for the crimes of Hitler and the intolerance of Europe by becoming refugees themselves.

* * *

In the meantime, the Zionists were preparing themselves, more or less openly, for the eventual forceful eviction of the Arab population. In October, 1935, an incident occurred in the harbor of Jaffa, Palestine, during the unloading of a shipment consigned to Jewish merchants which revealed that the Zionists were

---

[103] Quoted in Royal Institute of International Affairs, p. 139.
[104] *Ibid.*, p. 143.

smuggling weapons into the country.[105] In a speech delivered on March 20, 1943, "Mr. Ben Gurion exhorted Jewish youth to prepare themselves for the fighting which would fall to their lot at the end of the war."[106] Jewish settlements were authorized by the mandatory government to keep armed guards, and extremist factions among the Zionists "more or less openly carried out military drills etc. They were also suspected with some reason of being in possession of arms more numerous and more lethal than the shotguns officially approved by the authorities."[107] Zionist terrorist organizations like the Irgun Zvai Leumi and the Stern Gang attacked other government installations for the purpose of stealing weapons. In 1943, trials of individual Jews accused of "a series of thefts of arms from military installations...revealed the existence of a large and wealthy Jewish organization for the systematic theft of arms and explosives from the British Army, not only in Palestine but throughout the Middle East."[108] When the Palestine police attempted to search Jewish villages for illegal weapons, they were accused by the Jewish Press of following in the footsteps of "Nazi Stormtroopers."[109]

* * *

To be sure, the Arabs of Palestine did not watch these developments passively; they protested and several times rebelled. Their protestations usually went unheard,

---

[105] Marlowe, p. 144.
[106] Royal Institute of International Affairs, p. 137.
[107] Marlowe, p. 136.
[108] Royal Institute of International Affairs, p. 137.
[109] *Ibid.*, pp. 136-137.

and when they were heard they were branded as heartless indifference to the plight of the Jews of Europe. The world was not ready or willing to recognize these protests for what they were: the protests of a people who were being deprived of the right to live in their ancestral land. Their rebellions were crushed, and they were denied the right of self-defense.

During the 1936-1939 Arab rebellion against British rule in Palestine, the possession of weapons was made a capital crime, and the country was placed under martial law and ruled by decree. The Arabs of Palestine were even deprived of their political leadership. Just before the Second World War, the Arabs of Palestine were asked to send a delegation to the London Conference which was to be held by Arab, Jewish, and British representatives. Jamal Husseini, who "appeared to be the only personality generally acceptable as a leader " was in exile, and the Mandatory government refused to allow him to return to Palestine or even to Egypt where he could be reached for consultation during the conference. All petitions to this effect submitted by Palestine's Arabs to the Mandatory government were rejected.[110]

The spirit of the preceding story of the British Mandate over Palestine was captured by a British author who wrote: "Great Britain did not come to Palestine to preside behind the scales of justice; she came to Palestine and stayed there for strategical and imperialist reasons."[111] These reasons made it expedient for Britain to

---

[110] *Ibid.*, p. 135.
[111] Marlowe, p. 55.

issue the Balfour Declaration, which gave it a pretext for securing from the Allies a Mandate for Palestine. They made it expedient for Britain to create a non-existent Arab-Jewish conflict which it could, and did, use as a "justification" for remaining in Palestine as long as it's "strategical and imperialist" objectives required.

When these objectives no longer required British control of Palestine, Britain was ready to evacuate the country leaving in its wake the conflict and the hostility which, for the first time in history, have come to characterize Arab-Jewish relations. On April 2, 1947, the British government informed the Secretary General of the United Nations that it was unable to reconcile the Arab-Jewish dispute, and it requested the convening of a special session of the international organization for the purpose of constituting and instructing a special committee to prepare a preliminary study of the problem to be submitted to the regular session of the General Assembly.

CHAPTER 5 - THE PROBLEM

What was the problem which Britain failed to solve and sought the assistance of the United Nations in solving? It was shown in the previous chapters that prior to the end of the First World War there was no Arab-Jewish conflict in Palestine. The Zionist scheme for the establishment of a Jewish state in Palestine did not and could not, in itself, constitute an Arab-Jewish dispute. An attempt to implement that scheme, however, was quite a different matter, because it obviously meant the infringement upon the historical rights of the Arabs of Palestine by their eviction from their country.

The issuance of the Balfour Declaration and the implementation of its pro-Zionist provisions during British rule of Palestine were bringing this threat of eviction into reality. The British Mandate had increased the Jewish population, mainly by immigration, from less than one-tenth to about one-third of the total population of the country. It established Hebrew as an official language, as were Arabic and English. It enabled and recognized the Zionist Organization (later, the Jewish Agency) to be a semi-governmental authority, a sort of government within a government.

65

In short, the British Mandate had brought the Zionists so close to the fulfillment of their goal that they clung to it more tenaciously and became determined to accept nothing less than a Jewish state. On the other hand, British administration of Palestine had convinced its Arab population beyond the shadow of doubt, and more than ever before, that nothing short of immediate independence could save them from being reduced to a minority within their own country or guarantee them the right to continue to live in their ancestral home.

What the problem of Palestine boiled down to, then, was this: the Arab majority was seeking the country's independence while they were still a majority, and the Jewish minority was seeking a formula by which it would have the means of assuring the continuation of large-scale Jewish immigration in order to achieve a numerical majority as a prelude to the establishment of a Jewish state. The aims of the Arab majority and the Jewish minority were obviously incompatible and mutually exclusive. In this predicament, Palestine was not a novel or unique example in human history, past or present. It is rather the rule than the exception to encounter in societies with numerically significant minorities a clash of aims and demands.

Whereas in other "civilized" communities such conflicts are reconciled on the basis of the principle of majority rule which takes into consideration the legitimate rights and interests of the minority as a group and/or as individuals, Palestine was to be treated as an exception. The British government in Palestine had chosen to wait for the emergence of a solution acceptable to both sides. Pro-Zionist governments and press were urging the British government not to accept a solution which did not enjoy the acceptance of the *minority.*

In other words, in the case of Palestine, the voice of the Jewish minority was to be given a weight at least equal to the voice of the Arab majority in determining the future government of the country. Some Zionist writers had formulated an ideological justification for such an arrangement. After defining the term "nation" in a way which would qualify Jewish minorities wherever they lived as nations within nations, one such writer concluded by saying: "When several nations [i.e., several ethnic minority groups] live together in the same country or are united into one state, they must have *equal political rights without regard to their numerical strength.*"[112] Such a formula amounted to minority rule or, at best, to giving the minority the right to veto the choice of the majority. It goes without saying that neither Britain nor any other country on earth was or is willing to give such disproportionate "right" to *its* Jewish minority.

From the preceding paragraphs, it becomes obvious that if the problem of Palestine were presented to the world as it actually was, the problem of a minority group seeking to impose its demands upon the rest of the population, the Jewish-Zionist case would have been recognized to be untenable. Other factors had to be, and were, injected into the picture which confused it and

---

[112] Joseph Heller, *The Zionist Idea.* (New York: Schocken Books, 1949), p. 21. (Italics *added*). It would be instructive perhaps to apply the "principle" to the United States and to attempt to trace the consequences of its application to the country's political system.

altered its appearance. Hitler, the concentration camps, and anti-Semitism — all of which were factors alien to Palestine and to its problem — were drawn into the arena and woven so intricately in the fabric of the Palestine question by Zionist and Zionist-oriented press that the real issue disappeared out of sight.

By the time the question of Palestine appeared on the agenda of the United Nations General Assembly in 1947, the Zionists had told and retold the story of Hitler's gas chambers so frequently and so effectively that the uppermost thought in the minds of the delegates who assembled to pass judgement in the case of Palestine was, not to attempt to work out an equitable solution to the problem before them, but to answer the question: what can be done for the Jews? The fact that the displaced person problem in Europe was "peripheral to the central issue of the future government of Palestine"[113] was ignored, and the rights and the wishes of the Arabs of Palestine — who still constituted two-thirds of the country's population — were treated as if they were peripheral or entirely irrelevant. Palestine's Arabs were looked upon as if they were an inconvenience, the absence of which would have made a solution to the "Jewish problem" easier. This confusion of Palestine's problem with the displaced persons question had its effects not only upon the little interested and less informed "world public opinion" but also upon the governments which professed an interest in Palestine's difficulties.

---

[113] Robert E. Riggs, *Politics in the United Nations* (Urbana: The University of Illinois Press, 1958), pp. 56-57.

An illuminating example of the influence of this maneuver to present the question of Palestine as a mere aspect of the worldwide "Jewish problem" could be seen in the experience of the Anglo-American Committee of Inquiry on Palestine which was set up in 1946. An American member of the committee had written a book dealing with its work which made it quite clear that the primary preoccupation of the British and American governments was, not to deal with the problem of Palestine on its own merits, but to investigate the possibility of using Palestine as a possible solution to the "Jewish problem." The Committee was not to concern itself with the opinions or wishes of the people who made Palestine their home because, were that the case, "the Arab case might have been unanswerable."[114] Instead, the Committee's terms of reference directed it to find out what could be done with Palestine in order to assure the protection of "Jews menaced by persecution."[115] It was little wonder, then, that a committee set up for the purpose of studying the problem of Palestine was debating a "solution" as soon as it landed in Europe and saw displaced persons' camps, and before it even set foot on the soil of Palestine!

While still in New York, and before the Committee sailed to Palestine, the same American member had held a press conference in which he stated that the displaced persons' camps "had to be cleared out. The displaced persons must be permitted to go where they wanted to go,

---

[114] Crum, p. 23.
[115] *Ibid.*

and if that was Palestine, so be it."[116] In other words, the committee on Palestine was not only doing its research thousands of miles away from the country, but some of its members had already reached their verdict before they even got there! This was the effect of grafting the "Jewish problem" on the question of Palestine.

It was within this frame of mind that the question was discussed when the British government announced its inability to solve it and threw the responsibility on the yet untested shoulders of the United Nations.

---

[116] *Ibid.*

PART TWO

THE HARVEST OF SHAME

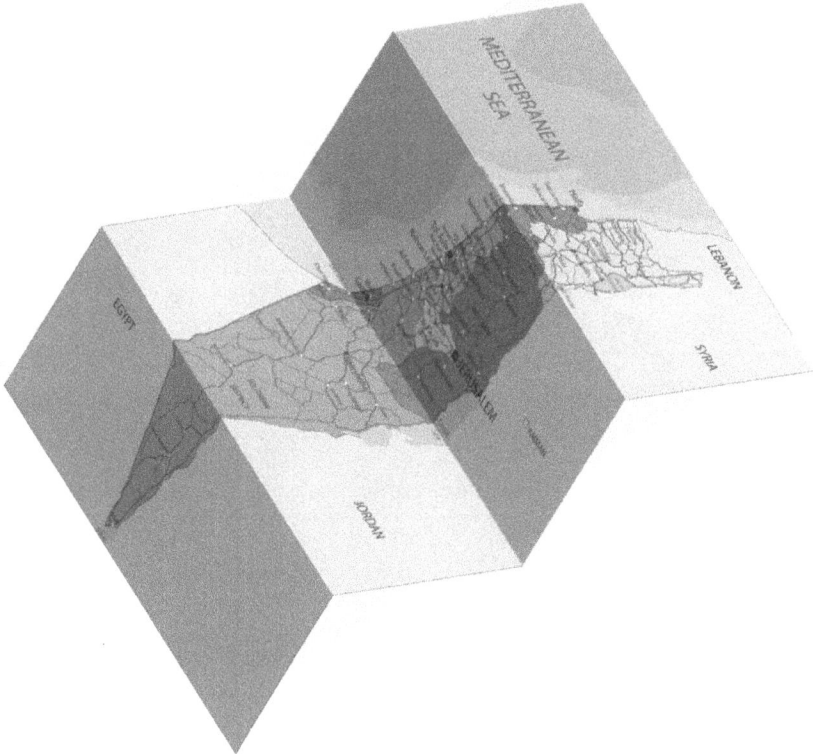

CHAPTER 6 - PARTITION

Ironic as this may sound, the rise of Hitler and his attempt to exterminate the Jews of Europe was one of the most important causes of the triumph of Zionism and the eventual establishment of a Jewish state in Palestine. An American Zionist said that "without the DP's [displaced persons], the Jewish state might never have come into being."[117] A similar remark was made by a leading figure of the Zionist movement who subsequently became the leader of the second largest political party in Israel and a member of the Israeli parliament and cabinet. He observed that "by a grim and ghastly irony, the German plan [to exterminate the Jews] helped to fulfill — by means unexpected and gruesome — the fundamental plan for Eretz Israel."[118]

Hitler's concentration camps not only resulted in an almost complete conversion of Jews to Zionism, but they gained for the Zionists wide support which otherwise would not have been possible. Moreover, they firmly established the Jews in the popular mind as the underdogs of the twentieth century. The immense loss of the Jews almost placed them beyond criticism and helped

---

[117] Marie Syrkin, *Golda Meir: Woman With a Cause.* (New York: G.P. Putnam's Sons, 1963), p. 251.

[118] Menahem Begin, *The Revolt: Story of the Irgun.* (New York: Henry Shuman, 1951), p. 29.

create a myth that they could do no wrong. Who would dare risk being called anti-Semitic now that Hitler's concentration camps had elevated the charge to the rank of a crime of the gravest nature? The Zionists were fully aware of all this, and they used it to their best advantage. But sympathy was not the Zionists' objectives; it was only an indispensable means to it. Their objective was the establishment of their control over Palestine. They were aware of the fact that there would be people who would not accept the suffering of European Jewry as sufficient justification for trampling upon the rights of the Arab people of Palestine and would protest that two wrongs do not make a right. And there *were* people who believed that "there is no equity in the aggression represented in seizing land from peoples who have inhabited it for two thousand years, and turning it over to a set of invaders just because these are persecuted in Europe."[119]

So they falsified both history and contemporary realities in order to propagate the belief that Zionist control of Palestine represented neither a transgression upon the historical right of the Arab people nor an abridgment of their present rights. The Zionists and their supporters have encouraged various misconceptions about Palestine's history, old and modern, which tended to give credence to Jewish claims in Palestine.

Whenever they discussed the history of Palestine, they began it with the period during which the Jews were

---

[119] From a letter to Sumner Welles, former Secretary of State, quoted in his book *We Need Not Fail*. (Boston: Houghton Mifflin Co., 1948), p. 1.

in occupation of the Holy Land[120] in order to foster the belief that the Jews were the original people of Palestine. This, of course, is erroneous. The Jews came to Palestine as conquerors, and their presence was imposed upon a people who had already been living there.[121] Zionists and their supporters distorted the history of Palestine to minimize the significance and even the duration of Arab presence in the country. In one case, the history of Palestine was summed up as follows:

> The Roman devastation of Palestine in 135 A.D. ended some twelve hundred years of Jewish history in that land, with the slaughter or expulsion of most of the Jews. Palestine then became successively a part of the Roman and Byzantine Empires. Subsequently it was occupied for three centuries by the Arabs. After these were conquered by the Seljuk Turks, Palestine passed from the hands of one conqueror to those of another. For almost a hundred years after 1095 A.D. it was under the control of the Crusaders. But from the year 1517 A.D., when the Ottoman Turks conquered it, until the close of the First World War, Palestine was continuously a province of the Turkish Empire. Except for the Egyptians and some of the other peoples of North Africa, none of the present Arab nations obtained their freedom from Turkish rule until Turkey was defeated by the Allies in the First World War.

---

[120] *Ibid.*, p. vii, p. 1.
[121] Emmanuel Anati, *Palestine Before the Hebrews*, (New York: Alfred A. Knopf, 1963).

On August 10, 1920, the victorious Allies compelled Turkey to sign the peace Treaty of Sevres. By the terms of that treaty Turkey was forced to cede to the Allies her province of Palestine. Under international law Palestine thus became subject to whatever disposal the Allies might decide to make of its inhabitants and territory.[122]

The implication of this presentation, of course, is that Palestine was an Arab land for only 300 years, and that throughout the rest of its history it was a province of one people or another. What this "history" does not make clear is *the fact that throughout this entire time, the Arab people remained in continuous habitation of Palestine and never lost their prescriptive right to the land.* The Arabs did not lose their right to Palestine when they became subjected to foreign rule. No people lose their right to their country by being ruled by a foreign power. It is a well-known fact that the Jews were not always free and sovereign when they had a Kingdom in Palestine. During the time of Christ, for example, Palestine was a province of Rome. How is it, then, that the period of Roman rule over "Jewish Palestine" can be counted as a part of Jewish history in Palestine, but foreign rule over "Arab Palestine" does not count as a part of Arab history in it? The fallacy is so apparent that this writer finds it difficult to believe that such a distortion is a result of misunderstanding and not deliberate.

---

[122] Welles, pp. 1-2.

Another Zionist sympathizer who, as a member of the United Nations Committee on Palestine and as the chief delegate of his country to the United Nations, helped to determine the fate of Palestine, echoed this often-used fallacious argument and concluded that the Arabs historic connection with Palestine "was so brief as to be the duration of a lightning flash, historically."[123] This same astute observer stated that Arab historical claims to Palestine suffered from the fact that "Palestine had never been an Arab sovereign state."[124] The fact that Palestine constituted a part of a larger Arab state for many centuries, according to this absurd interpretation of history, disqualifies it from being Arab territory! Using this analysis California could not be considered American territory because it has never been an independent and sovereign American state.

This distortion of Palestine's history was paralleled by a distortion of contemporary conditions there. The Zionists pictured Palestine as being a sparsely populated land inhabited by a backward people who heartlessly opposed the amelioration of the tragic conditions of the remnants of European Jewry. The fact that the Arab people had extremely limited access to the media of communications meant that the public, and especially the American public, remained almost totally unfamiliar with the Arab side of the story while it was incessantly bombarded with Zionist propaganda. Arab protests that

---

[123] Jorge Garcia-Granados, *The Birth of Israel*. (New York: Alfred A. Knopf, 1948), p. 63.
[124] *Ibid.*

they were being slandered and misrepresented reached only a few ears. In vain did they protest that throughout their history, the Arabs had offered refuge to Jews persecuted in other lands. They pointed out that their objection was to being made to shoulder the *entire* burden of the Jewish problem while other countries did nothing except lecture the Arab people about humanitarianism.[125] Moreover, the Arabs pointed out the fact that the Zionists were using the misfortune of their European brethren in order to gain control of Palestine. The Secretary General of the Arab League, in his testimony before the Anglo-American Committee of Inquiry, expressed Arab apprehensions this way:

> The Zionist, the new Jew, wants to dominate and he pretends that he has got a particular civilizing mission with which he returns to a backward, degenerate race in order to put the elements of progress into an area which has no progress. Well, that has been the pretension of every power that wanted to colonize and aimed at domination. The excuse has always been that the people are backward and that he has got a human mission to put them forward... The Arabs simply stand and say NO! We are not reactionary, and we are not backward. Even if we are ignorant, the difference between ignorance and knowledge is ten years in

---

[125] "No one in Washington denied that one of the main obstacles in the way of Arab acceptance of a measure of Jewish immigration into Palestine was the refusal of the Western democracies to open their doors to the refugees." Crossman, *Palestine Mission: A Personal Record.* p. 45.

school. We are a living, vitally strong nation; we are in our renaissance; we are producing as many children as any nation in the world. We still have our brains. We have a heritage of civilization and spiritual life. We are not going to allow ourselves to be controlled either by great nations or small nations or dispersed nations.[126]

It is interesting to note that in their effort to justify their aims in Palestine, the Zionists took a leaf out of Hitler's book. He justified his demands for a German *lebensraum* on much the same basis: "For as matters stand," Hitler wrote in *Mein Kampf,* "there are at the present time on this earth immense areas of unused soil, only waiting for the men to till them...this soil exists for the people which possesses the force to take it and the industry to cultivate it."[127]

Hitler was condemned for such views; the Zionists were condoned for them.

Zionist distortion of the facts, of course, was not the only explanation for the wide support which they received for their cause. The idea of a resurrected Jewish nation appealed to the religious conception of many people in the Christian world. It was previously shown that the Balfour Declaration found support among certain religious circles in Britain because it seemed to be in line with the Biblical prophecy concerning the "return" of the Jews to Palestine. Similarly, certain religious groups in the

---

[126] Quoted in Crossman, *Palestine Mission,* p. 110.

[127] Adolf Hitler, *Mein Kampf,* tr by Ralph Manheim, (Boston: Houghton Mifflin, 1943), p. 134.

United States were receptive to the Zionist idea for the same reason. During its investigation of the problem of Palestine after the end of the Second World War, the Anglo-American Committee of Inquiry found that "the Federal Council of the Churches of Christ in America was fervently Zionist, basing its argument on the fundamentalist assertion that the Biblical prophecy of a Jewish return to Zion before the Second Coming must be fulfilled."[128]

Another explanation for the support which the Zionists received was the fact that a Jewish state which would accommodate a large number of Jewish refugees would save many countries from the embarrassment of having to cope with the problem themselves.

The Peel Commission of 1936 recommended the partition of Palestine and the establishment of a Jewish state in a part of its territory. "The hope that partition would make possible the admission of a greater number of Jews into Palestine was its chief commendation in the eyes of representatives alike of those countries which have a large number and unpopular Jewish population and of those which were likely to be embarrassed by an influx of refugees."[129] So the Zionists had several factors working in their favor.

But of all these factors, they realized that the recent disclosure of Nazi atrocities was their chief asset. But they were not satisfied that the tragedy which befell their European co- religionists was sufficient. Their

---

[128] Crossman, *Palestine Mission,* pp. 41-42.
[129] Royal Institute, p. 108.

determination to squeeze every last drop of propaganda out of the tragedy led the Zionists to exaggeration and then to the Commission of crimes against their own people!

Hitler's war was waged against humanity, yet it was pictured as if it were only an aggression against the Jews. Six million Jews were massacred during the war, the Zionists never tired of reminding the world, as if the tens of millions of European dead hardly mattered. Moreover, the displaced persons were made to appear synonymous with Jewish refugees "although the Jews were only a tiny fraction of the total number of D. P.'s."[130]

The Zionists also sent their agents to round up Jews from all over Europe and to bring them to displaced persons camps in order to exaggerate the refugee problem. When a British general disclosed this fact, he aroused indignation in the United States and was "assailed in every editorial."[131] The Anglo-American Committee of Inquiry, however, had found evidence to indicate that "what the general had said was a great deal less than the truth."[132] The actual tragedy and even the exaggeration of its meaning and extent still failed to satiate Zionist greed for propagandist gains.

The sinking of the *Patria* off the coast of Palestine showed that the Zionists placed no limit to the lengths they were prepared to go in their quest for sympathy through tear-jerking techniques. After the end of the war,

---

[130] Crossman, *Palestine Mission*, pp. 175-176.
[131] *Ibid.*, p. 82.
[132] *Ibid.*, pp. 82-84.

ships crowded with the illegal immigrants began to arrive in Palestine. One such ship was the *Patria*. When Palestine authorities refused to permit illegal entry of refugees into the country, Zionist terrorists planted a bomb in the ship to prevent it from sailing. The bomb exploded and resulted in the sinking of the ship and the loss of more than 200 lives.[133]

In short, Zionist propagandists so distorted the facts about Palestine, and so effectively used the misfortune of European Jewry that they created a highly charged emotional atmosphere which precluded the possibility that the Arab case would get a fair hearing. The Zionists saw to it that the public viewed Palestine through a haze of tears which clouded its vision. It became almost sacrilegious to think of such a thing as Arab rights, and it became almost inhumane to think that there was such a thing as an Arab side of this story which perhaps merited consideration.

This type of atmosphere led not only to the suffocation of the truth about Palestine, but to the involvement of the United States in one of the most unjust exercises of influence in the country's entire history. It caused the United States government to pursue a policy which was to result in a major human tragedy to the detriment of its national interests.

When the Second World War ended, the American Jewish community emerged as the undisputed leader of world Jewry. The world Zionist movement's center of power shifted from Europe to the United States. This shift

---

[133] Begin, p. 35. Begin blames the crime on the Haganah.

was caused by the fact that European Jewry was nearly decimated, while the American Jewish community not only remained intact but also experienced a large-scale conversion to Zionism. Nazism seemed to refute the argument that assimilation was the solution to the Jewish problem and to confirm the Zionist thesis that "Anti-Semitism... is a bacillus which every Gentile carries with him wherever he goes and however he denies it."[134] This strengthening of the American Zionist movement, accompanied by the belief that American Jews occupied a pivotal position in American presidential politics, resulted in the fact that Palestine became a domestic issue in American politics. Since Americans knew very little about the problem of Palestine and cared less about the outcome of the struggle there, the Zionists were practically the only segment of the population which molded public opinion on that issue. Their opinion on Palestine became almost synonymous with American public opinion. An alliance emerged between the Zionists and the vote seekers.

American politicians have always been harassed by pressures from all types of special interests and minority groups. President Wilson was subjected to so much pressure to intervene in Mexico on behalf of investors whose property was endangered by the Mexican revolution that he said: "I sometimes have to pause and remind myself that I am President of the whole United States and not merely of a few property holders in the

---

[134] Chaim Weizmann, first president of Israel, was quoted in Crossman, *A Nation Reborn,* pp. 14-15.

Republic of Mexico."[135] Some presidents resisted these pressures better than others. Harry S. Truman's capitulation to Zionist pressure was complete. He not only disregarded the advice of his political and military advisors by giving complete support to the Zionists, but he employed the United States' considerable influence in the United Nations of 1947 to guarantee their success when the international organization sought a solution to the problem of Palestine.

It should be pointed out that Russia also made its contribution. It played an important part, both in the General Assembly and in the Security Council, in securing the passage of the partition resolution. Stalinist Russia was, of course, delighted to see the British Empire disappear, and it seized every opportunity to hasten the process. The establishment of a Jewish state in Palestine meant Britain's withdrawal from the country. Moreover, a Jewish state in Palestine, and the support which that state was bound to receive from the Western powers — especially the United States — would create a tremendous resentment against the West in the whole Arab world. What better way was there for Russia to endanger Western interests in the Middle East?

The Zionists realized this fact. In 1903 Theodor Herzl said that the Zionists would establish a state in Palestine "not from the goodwill but from the jealousy of the Powers."[136] Early in 1946, a Zionist leader stated the same

---

[135] Rear Admiral Cary T. Grayson, *Woodrow Wilson: An Intimate Memoir*, (New York: Holt, Rinehart and Winston, 1960), p. 30.
[136] See Chapter Two, footnote 26.

idea by saying : "*we say with absolute confidence that Russia too will help in making Eretz Israel [Palestine] a Jewish state...*[Russia] wants the fight of the Jewish people against the British Mandatory."[137] Events were to prove them right. When the question of Palestine was placed on the agenda of the General Assembly, the Soviet Union was to be one of the most uncompromising proponents of partition.

On April 2, 1947, the British government finally conceded its failure to cope with the problem which its espousal of Zionism had created in Palestine. On that date, it transmitted to the Secretary General of the United Nations a request for placing the question of Palestine on the agenda of the coming regular session of the General Assembly. It also requested that the Secretary General call a special session for the purpose of appointing a committee to study the problem and to prepare recommendations for its solution. The special session was called and met on April 28, 1947. It appointed a Special Committee on Palestine (UNSCOP) and adjourned. This committee consisted of representatives from Australia, Canada, Czechoslovakia, India, Iran, the Netherlands, Peru, Sweden, Uruguay, and Yugoslavia. After six weeks of investigation, including the inevitable visit to Europe's concentration camps, the committee submitted its findings on August 31, 1947. These findings resulted in two plans for solving the Arab-Jewish dispute over Palestine.

---

[137] Begin, p. 197. Italics in the original. Begin was at that time the commander of the Irgun Zvai Leumi terrorist group.

One plan, (endorsed by India, Iran, and Yugoslavia) recommended the establishment of a federal union. The rest of the committee members (excluding Australia which refused to endorse either plan) recommended the partition of Palestine into Arab and Jewish states with an economic union.

When the General Assembly met in regular session in the fall of 1947, it appointed an ad hoc committee on Palestine to consider the problem and the reports of UNSCOP. After slight modifications of the partition plan, the ad hoc committee accepted it. On November 26th, 1947, the partition plan was introduced in plenary session of the General Assembly the prospects of its approval looked dim, because it had failed to secure in the committee the two-thirds majority vote which important questions require for approval by the General Assembly.

The proponents of the partition, however, were determined to see it approved. The delegates and their governments were subjected to a campaign of pressure and intimidation which was never equaled before or since. The late James Forrestal, former U.S. Secretary of Defense, wrote in his diaries that "the methods that had been used...to bring coercion and duress on other nations in the General Assembly bordered closely onto scandal."[138]

President Truman's decision to put the United States' full influence behind the Zionist case for a Jewish state has been attributed to his eagerness to secure Jewish

---

[138] Walter Millis, ed., *The Forrestal Diaries,* (New York: The Viking Press, 1951), p. 363.

votes. When Mr. Truman demanded that the British government allow the immediate entry of 100,000 Jews into Palestine after the end of the Second World War, Ernest Bevan—then British Prime Minister—"publicly accused Mr. Truman of playing politics for the sake of the Jewish votes in New York."[139] Even Zionist sympathizers agreed that Mr. Truman's support for a Jewish state was politically motivated.[140]

One may argue that the American Jewish community is too small a minority to sway a presidential election. Moreover, it can be said that Jewish voters are not so united in their views as to create such a thing as a "Jewish vote." Both of these objections would be valid. However, the fact that it is not unlikely that a candidate would win or lose the election by a margin of only a few hundred thousand votes gives disproportionate influence to a minority group. Even when this fact is disregarded, it remains true that a small minority of voters would have considerable influence if the candidates only *thought* the minority could affect the outcome of the election. The point, therefore, is that whether there is or there is not a "Jewish vote" which could sway a presidential election is immaterial. The important thing is that Mr. Truman evidently believed that there was such a thing as a Jewish vote, and he acted in a manner which would secure that vote for him.

During hearings on American foreign policy in the Middle East, a former American ambassador testified that

---

[139] Crossman, *A Nation Reborn*, p. 80.
[140] Welles, p. 80.

87

Mr. Truman admitted that his decision to support the Zionist view in the Arab-Israeli dispute was motivated by Mr. Truman's quest for the "Jewish vote." When his advisors pointed out to him that such partiality to the Zionist cause would harm American interests in the Middle East, he replied by saying:

> I am sorry, gentleman, but I have to answer hundreds of thousands who are anxious for the success of Zionism; I do not have hundreds of thousands of Arabs among my constituents.[141]

So, the pressure was turned on. A former assistant Secretary of State highly sympathetic to the Zionist cause had said that "By direct order of the White House every form of pressure, direct and indirect, was brought to bear by American officials upon those countries outside the Moslem world that were known to be either uncertain or opposed to partition. Representatives or intermediates were employed by the White House to make sure that the necessary majority would at length be secured."[142]

Several countries, including Cuba, Iran, Pakistan, and Chile, protested the pressure to which they were being subjected by American officials. Chile, which supported partition in the ad hoc committee was so resentful of that pressure that it abstained instead of voting for partition when the vote was called for in the

---

[141] U.S. Senate, Committee on Foreign Relations, 86th Congress, 1st Session. June 15, 1959, p.69.
[142] Wells, p. 63.

General Assembly.[143] But the fact pressure exerted on members of the United Nations was not successful in all cases does not mean that it produced no support for the Zionist cause. "The switch of Haiti and the Philippines from a negative position to a vote for partition was doubtless influenced in some degree by pressure from [U.S.] official sources."[144] The delegate from the Philippines had spoken against partition in committee then voted for it in plenary session. In addition to the pressures exerted on his delegation in New York, his government was sent a telegram by 26 pro-Zionist Senators and Supreme Court justices urging it to change its view, and it did."[145] Also, "many persons having official connections with the United States government worked actively to promote the Zionist cause. As a result, the line between official and non-official pressure at times became extremely thin."[146]

Adolph A. Berle, former Assistant Secretary of State, used his influence with the Haitian government to support partition. It did. Harvey Firestone, with his extensive business interests in Liberia, personally

---

[143] U. S. pressure was so instrumental in the passage of the partition resolution that non-Zionists writers on the problem of Palestine almost always devote considerable attention to it. For example, see Alfred M Lilienthal, *What Price Israel.* (Henry Regnery Company, 1953), pp. 48-73. But this account relies primarily on Riggs, *Politics in the United Nations.*

[144] *Ibid.*

[145] *Ibid.*

[146] *Ibid.*

telephoned the Liberian government urging it to support partition, and it did.[147]

A study of United States' influence on the passage of the partition resolution concluded that the pressure exerted "without doubt, saved the partition resolution from defeat."[148] The pressures exerted were evidently so severe and so varied that the same study could only qualify them by saying that "It is not likely...that pressure by the United States government extended as far as direct threats and bribes."[149]

The Zionists, however, did not completely rely on the United States government to pull their chestnuts from the fire, even though it was doing a satisfactory job. Their own pressure techniques prompted a student of that episode to observe: "Perhaps the most notorious case of pressure from private and non-governmental interests was the highly effective Zionist campaign for partition of Palestine in 1947."[150] By November 29, 1947, enough votes were lined up behind partition to secure its passage. The resolution, recommending the establishment of an Arab state, a Jewish state, and an internationalized area centering around Jerusalem was approved.

This birth certificate of the state of Israel, nurtured by falsification and distortion, and born of intrigue and the blatant misuse of power, was and is still pictured as the supreme manifestation of the will of mankind. As in the case of other decrees and declarations which favored

---

[147] *Ibid.*
[148] *Ibid.*
[149] *Ibid.*
[150] *Ibid.*

their cause, the Zionists have sought to clothe the resolution with an aura of inviolable sanctity by claiming for it noble and moral motivations. Mr. Ben Gurion said that the partition resolution gave "supreme international sanction"[151] to the establishment of a Jewish state. A sympathizer, writing in defense of the resolution in 1949, expressed the untenable belief that the United Nations General Assembly "speaks for the organized moral opinion of all peoples."[152]

To add insult to injury, the partition resolution was much too favorable to the Zionists in defining the respective areas allotted to the Arab and Jewish states which it envisioned. Even when Palestine's partition and the methods used to secure it are not considered, the resolution would still be an act of grave injustice if only on the grounds that it so favored the Zionists at the expense of Palestine's Arab population.

The resolution allocated to the "Jewish state" 56.47% of the total area of Palestine, although the Jewish population of the country was only one-third of the total. The Arab people, who comprised two-thirds of the population, were allocated 42.88%. The rest of the area (.65%) was allocated for the International Zone.[153] The extent of the inequity becomes even more apparent when one considers the fact that but for a small percentage, the area given to the Jewish state consisted of Arab-owned

---

[151] David Ben Gurion, *Israel: Years of Challenge.* (New York: Holt, Rinehart and Winston, 19663), p. 29.

[152] Welles, p. 48.

[153] Sami Hadawi, *Land Ownership in Palestine.*(New York: The Palestine Arab Refugee Office, January 1957).

land. A study of land ownership in Palestine, based on Palestine government records and compiled by the Chief of the Land Taxation Section before the withdrawal of Britain from the country, shows that only 9.38% of the land given to the Jewish state was Jewish owned.[154]

If this expropriation of the property of the Arabic people of Palestine to atone for Hitler's sins constitute "the organized moral opinion of all peoples," then something is undoubtedly amiss with contemporary international morality. The Arab people's protests against the injustice of the act were and are still depicted as the unreasonable intransigence of rampant nationalism.

The Zionists were not quite satisfied with their victory in the United Nations. The Executive Committee of the Jewish Agency, the official spokesman of Palestine's Jewish minority, announced its willingness to "sacrifice" and accept the partition resolution as an "irreducible minimum." "The extremist, however, rejected the decision that had been reached, and insisted that they would never be satisfied until the Jewish people controlled the whole of Palestine."[155]

As events unfolded, it became apparent that while Zionist official spokesmen gave their grudging acceptance of the partition resolution, the extremists were preparing to carry out their plans for the Jewish domination of all of Palestine. As a result, Palestine became embroiled in violence the end of which is not yet in sight. It became a

---

[154] *Ibid.*, p. 19. Of the territory allocated to the Arab state only 0.84% was Jewish owned.

[155] Welles, p. 65.

powder keg ever-ready to be ignited, and its people were made a nation of refugees.

CHAPTER 7 - WAR

> If our dreams of Zionism are to end in the smoke of assassin's pistols and our labours for its future are to produce a new set of gangsters worthy of Nazi Germany, many like myself will have to reconsider the position which we have maintained so consistently and so long in the past.
>
> — Winston Churchill

One of the most frequently overlooked facts of life is that an underdog often becomes a nuisance and even a menace by abusing the sympathy which his misfortune tends to generate for him in the hearts of other people. Like a sick or newly orphaned child, he lives behind a shield of pity which often enables him to get away with actions which are normally punishable.

In 1947-1949 the Jews of Palestine were in such a position, and they knew it. Hitler's concentration camps and gas chambers were still contemporary episodes and had not yet become a part of history. The world had not yet overcome the shock of recent revelations of Nazi crimes, and interest in the "Jewish problem" was still intense and widespread. This interest encouraged Jewish elements in Palestine to be uncompromising in their aims and unscrupulous in their methods. It certainly emboldened Jewish terrorists during the last years of the British mandate in their armed raids on government installations for the purpose of gathering weapons and ammunitions for their coming assault upon the Arab population of Palestine. On several occasions since then, this stereotype of the Jew as the oppressed rather than the oppressor has helped Israel engage in the unrestrained use of violence and in expansionism with impunity.

Zionist leaders realized the benefits they could derive from this psychological shelter. This fact was made evident, for example, by Menachim Begin who was, during the Mandate, the commander of the Irgun Zvai Leumi terrorist group, and who later became a political party leader, a member of the Knesset, and a member of the Israeli Cabinet during the Arab-Israeli war in June, 1967. When the more cautious elements in the Jewish community warned Begin that the excesses of his terrorist group during the last years of the British Mandate over Palestine might cause the Zionist movement to lose some of its supporters, and might provoke British retaliation against the country's Jewish minority, the Irgun commander dismissed the warning by saying:

It is a fact that no partisan struggle had been so publicized throughout the world as ours. While our revolt was in progress, a number of battles of considerable magnitude were fought in the Greek mountains. They were accorded but a few lines in the world's press. The reports of our operations, under screaming headlines, covered the front pages of newspapers everywhere, particularly in the United States.[156]

This publicity, he concluded, had "built a kind of invisible lifebelt around the Jewish population."[157]

When the United Nations General Assembly passed a resolution recommending the partition of Palestine on November 29, 1947, the Jews of Palestine (sheltered by the-underdog-can-do-no-wrong myth) proceeded to commit one of the major crimes of recent history. They terrorized and robbed a disarmed people of their land and their homes, and they turned them into a nation of refugees without being brought to book for it. Moreover, by so doing they were hailed as heroes.

As in the case of all previous phases of the Arab-Jewish conflict over Palestine, the Zionist point of view and interpretation of the Arab-Israeli war has been so widely disseminated that it has gained a much greater acceptance than is warranted by the facts. This process was helped by certain popular works of fiction, like *Exodus*, which somehow are passed off as history. The Jewish interpretation of the Arab-Israeli war of 1947-1949 is as simple as it is misleading. Briefly, it may be summarized as follows:

When the United Nations passed the partition resolution in 1947, the Arabs states announced their intention to oppose its implementation, by force if necessary. When the British completed their withdrawal from Palestine on May 15, 1948, and a Jewish state was

---

[156] Begin, p. 55.
[157] *Ibid.*

proclaimed, the regular Arab armies, which had been poised at the borders of Palestine waiting for Britain to withdraw, pounced on the infant state with the intention of killing it in its cradle. To everyone's surprise, the few hundred thousand Jews in Palestine — in a heroic act of self-defense — managed not only to repulse the Arab invasion, but to push the Arabs back and enlarge the territory of the Jewish state.

There is sufficient evidence to show that it was not a war of self-defense that the Jews of Palestine were engaged in, but an assault upon Palestine designed to bring under Jewish control the largest possible portion of the country. This fact is evident from both the words and the actions of the Jewish community in Palestine.

It is true that the Arabs refused to accept the United Nations recommendation on Palestine. In addition to the fact that the General Assembly's recommendation was the result of pressure tactics and not freely expressed, and in addition to the fact that its legality was challenged by the Arab states but was never allowed to reach the International Court of Justice for a ruling, it was so patently unjust to give the Jewish minority more than half the country when they owned less than 10% of the land, the Arab opposition to partition can be fully understandable. Opposition to a judgment is not ipso facto proof of guilt. On the contrary, a judgment can be so unjust — as the partition resolution was — that opposition to it is anything but a mark of guilt. It cannot be said that the true mother was guilty by rejecting Solomon's judgment to split the contested baby between the two "mothers" who claimed it.

The Jews, of course, can make no claim on virtue for having accepted the United Nations resolution. It is hardly a proof of generosity and of peaceful intentions to accept a judgment in one's own favor.[158]

Moreover, it is obvious that *the Jews were fully prepared to oppose the United Nations decision if that decision did not meet with their approval.* While the United Nations was still deliberating on the question of Palestine, a meeting took place between Menachim Begin, commander of the Irgun, and Moshe Sneh, a representative of Ben Gurion fully authorized to speak in his name. These two sides, therefore, represented both the "official" and the dissident opinions of Palestine's Jews. During the meeting, Moshe Sneh made it clear that the Jewish Agency, the official political organization of the Jewish community, was prepared to fight a United Nations decision which did not favor the Jews. If the United Nations decided on a "bad" partition, he said, "we shan't agree. And if they try to impose this scheme on us, we shall revolt. Ben Gurion is prepared for revolt."[159]

The dissidents, of course, were even more adamant. In their view no partition was good. They demanded that all of Palestine be given to the Jews. When the partition

---

[158] Such is Zionist mentality, however, that they did seek credit for accepting decisions partial to their cause. When the Anglo-American Committee of Inquiry recommended, among other things, the admission of 100,000 Jews into Palestine in 1946, the Jewish terrorist groups announced that "if the recommendations for the admission of one hundred thousand refugees were implemented no [terrorist] operations *liable to impede their entry would be carried out.*" Begin, pp. 201-202. Italics added.

[159] Begin, p. 139.

resolution was passed by the General Assembly, the Irgun actually rejected it and declared that the Jews were not bound to accept anything less than the whole of Palestine. "The partition of the Homeland is illegal," the Irgun declared. "It will never be recognized. The signature by institutions [i.e. the Jewish Agency] and individuals of the partition agreement is invalid. It will not bind the Jewish people. Jerusalem was and will forever be our capital. Eretz Israel [generally means Palestine, but in Irgun terminology means Palestine *and* Trans-Jordan] will be restored to the people of Israel. All of it. And forever."[160]

It is clear, therefore, that Jewish official acceptance of the partition resolution was not due to a greater attachment to peace than the Arabs had, but solely to the fact that partition was favorable to them while it was highly unfavorable to the Arabs. So how can the Arabs be condemned and the Jews condoned when the former did what the latter were fully prepared and determined to do if there had been a need for them to do it?

Another indication of Zionist mentality and of the double standards they used to judge their and Arab actions is shown by Israel's attitude toward Jerusalem. The United Nations resolution, on the basis of which a Jewish state in Palestine was built, provided that Jerusalem was to be internationalized. Israel, however, refused and still refuses to accept that part of the resolution. It justifies this particular violation of the

---

[160] Begin, p. 335.

resolution on the grounds that "Jerusalem was by decree of our history our Capital."[161]

More than 1300 years of continuous Arab habitation of Palestine "decree" that Palestine is an Arab land. If Jewish history can out-decree and overrule the United Nations, why can't Arab history do the same? Or is Jewish history more valid than other people's history?

* * *

The Jews not only misrepresented the Arabs' attempt to defend their rights as aggression, but they also misrepresented their own aggression as an act of self-defense. It is a matter of verifiable fact that the Jews of Palestine, not content with what the United Nations had proposed to give them in Palestine, seized upon the partition resolution as a pretext for controlling as much of Palestine as it was in their power to do so. With the partition resolution was passed, and several months before the Arab states intervened in Palestine, the Irgun expressed its unhappiness with partition, pointing out that war was coming to Palestine, and that "Such a war would be capable of changing everything..."[162] And of course it did.

The Jews succeeded in expanding the territory under their control from the 56.47% of the country which was allotted to them under the partition plan to about 80% which they occupied until the 1967 war when they again expanded.[163] Most of this expansion took place before

---

[161] Ben Gurion, *Israel: Years of Challenge*, p. 54.
[162] Begin, p. 335.
[163] Hadawi.

May 15, 1948; in other words, *before a single soldier of the Arab regular armies entered Palestine.*

For five and a half months, (from the time The United Nations recommended partition until the intervention of the Arab states in Palestine), the Arabs of Palestine were virtually defenseless against Jewish assault upon their lives and their property. The Jews, on the other hand, had maintained — in addition to the terrorist groups of the Irgun Zvai Leumi and the Stern Gang — a sizable force which existed and operated with the consent of the British Mandatory government, the Haganah. This armed organization was the military arm of the Jewish Agency under the leadership of Ben Gurion who was soon to become Israel's Prime Minister. These forces boasted men and armaments far beyond the knowledge of people who were surprised by the outcome of the Arab-Israeli war. The popular belief that Arab failure in Palestine was the outcome of Jewish valor and dedication stemmed from general ignorance of the military capabilities which the Jews of Palestine had built during the years of the British Mandate.

People in government, both in the United States and Britain knew better. A British expert on the Middle East told Richard Crossman, a British member of Parliament, even before the question of Palestine was taken to the United Nations that "the Haganah was the most powerful military force in the Middle East, apart from the British Army, and has completely transferred the balance of power." He added that, "if we [the British] withdrew from

Palestine, the Haganah would overrun the country and hold it for some years at least."[164]

Crossman later wrote that when he served on the Anglo-American Committee of Inquiry, he heard a British commander testify before the Committee that "the Haganah would be able without difficulty to hold any area allocated to the Jews under partition."[165]

Actually, this knowledge of the Haganah's military capability was considered by the Committee as adequate "justification" for recommending a pro-Jewish solution in Palestine. It is easier to implement a solution acceptable to the stronger party. The Haganah could easily enforce a pro-Jewish solution, "whereas large British reinforcements would be required to police any pro-Arab solution which involved the suppression of the Haganah. Deeply impressed by this testimony, we unanimously agreed on an interim solution, just—but only just— acceptable to the Jews."[166] Let those who do not believe that might makes right ponder this one!

The American government was also in possession of similar information regarding the relative military posture of the antagonists in Palestine. During a cabinet meeting on August 8, 1947, (before the British evacuation from Palestine), Secretary of State George Marshall reported that in the case of an Arab-Jewish war in Palestine, "in the first instance the Jews would be successful, owing to their superior weapons."[167] People in

164 Crossman, *Palestine Mission,* pp. 157-158.
165 Crossman, *A Nation Reborn.* p. 82.
166 *Ibid.*
167 Millis, p.303.

authority, who possessed information not accessible to the general public could not possibly have been surprised by the Arab's failure to defend Palestine.

* * *

This writer, who lived in Palestine at that time and speaks from personal knowledge of this aspect of Palestine's tragedy, finds certain writings on this subject simply puzzling. "It was notorious," said one writer, "that the Arabs in Palestine [were] getting all of the military equipment they needed from the neighboring Arab governments."[168] Where did he get his information? With the readers indulgence, I would like to interject a personal note. I lived in Qalqilya, a town of about 10,000 people until the refugees later swelled the number by several thousand. When the partition resolution led to violence, Qalqilya was almost completely disarmed. The reason I say "almost" is because about a score of people possessed antiquated rifles, World War I vintage, which they had kept well hidden since the 1936-1939 Arab rebellion against the Mandatory government. When violence seemed imminent in 1947, a few individuals were selected to purchase weapons from "outside." People who were financially able paid their money to the "purchasing committee," which departed on its mission.

When the committee returned, it turned out that the acquisitions consisted of a number of rifles of Italian, German, American, and British makes with a few thousand rounds of partly defective ammunition, some of which could not be replaced. The "weapons " had been

---

[168] Welles, p. 96.

103

bought in Libya from Bedouins who found them buried in the sands of the Sahara. They had been left there by Allied and Axis troops who fought in El Alamein and other North African campaigns. They were in very sad condition. In addition to the fact that some of the ammunition was defective, some of the rifles were not "battle worthy" by any stretch of imagination. I personally knew one person who bought one of these rifles and was killed in the first engagement where he used it. He fired one bullet out of that rifle, and the bolt got stuck leaving the man with a "metal stick" in the midst of battle. He was shot while trying to get the bolt unstuck by hitting it with a rock.

Qalqilya fared better than scores of smaller towns which found themselves in the front lines toward the end of 1947. With its obsolete rifles, Qalqilya was well armed in comparison with others. It actually found itself a protector of half a dozen villages around it, villages like Jaljulia and Kufr Kassem which had no weapons at all.

On the other hand, the Jews of Palestine—through the connections of Jewish communities in the United States and Europe—had no problems when it came to raising money or buying military equipment. When the hostilities began, Golda Myerson (now Meir) managed to raise $50 million in one fundraising campaign in the United States.[169]

In their writing about the war in Palestine, the Zionists also said that they lacked weapons. It must be pointed out, however, that when the Zionists spoke of

---

[169] Syrkin, p. 191.

their lack of weapons, they meant something entirely different from what the Arabs of Palestine meant when they spoke of the same handicap. To the Arabs of Palestine, a lack of weapons meant the availability of a few rusted rifles dug out of the sands of the Sahara, accompanied by irreplaceable, defective ammunition. To the Zionists, a lack of weapons meant the unavailability of field artillery, tanks, and military airplanes.

"What terrible disappointment our men suffered," the leader of the Irgun had said, "when they were sent to the battlefront with nothing more than Sten guns in their hands."[170] He may or may not have known that to the people of Qalqilya and the people of countless other Arab towns a Sten gun was such a rarity that it caused excitement for miles around.

When the Arab states intervened in Palestine the imbalance was somewhat rectified, but this intervention came several months after the hostilities began. During these months, the Arabs of Palestine alone and with almost bare hands stood facing a well-organized and armed adversary backed by the substantial resources of Jewish communities abroad. During these months, the Arabs of Palestine were subjected to a ruthless campaign of terrorism designed to drive them out of their homes to make room for the Jewish "exiles" who were supposedly waiting for a chance to "return to their homeland." Palestine had to be cleared of more than a million Arabs who had made it their home for more than thirteen centuries.

---

[170] Begin, p. 340.

People usually find it difficult to believe that the Jews, who had often been the victims of persecution, were themselves capable of cruel and criminal acts. But it is beyond question that Jewish atrocities against the Arabs of Palestine compare with the most deliberate collective crimes of all time. The most often mentioned example of Jewish crimes in Palestine is the Deir Yassin massacre of April 9, 1948. After most of the men folk had left the small Arab town for work, about 500 Jewish terrorists attacked it, destroyed it almost completely, massacred nearly every living soul they found there (including infants and a few pregnant women), and dumped the bodies in a well and covered them up with dirt. Representatives of the International Red Cross witnessed the removal of about 200 bodies from the well. Writing of this episode, Dr. Dov Joseph, a Palestinian Jew, said that the Deir Yassin massacre was "deliberate and unprovoked... There was no reason for the attack. It was a quiet village...which had not been involved in any attacks on Jewish areas."[171] A British Zionist Jew said that "the massacre of Deir Yassin was the darkest stain on the Jewish record throughout all the fighting."[172]

If the Deir Yassin massacre was "the darkest stain on the Jewish record," it was by no means the only one. Other acts of sheer terrorism, perhaps not as dramatic but certainly as reprehensible, were committed in many other

---

[171] Dov Joseph, *The Faithful City, The Siege of Jerusalem: 1948.* (New York: Simon and Schuster, 1960), p. 71.

[172] John Kimche, *The Seven Fallen Pillars.* (New York: Frederick A. Praeger, 1957), p.228. The Deir Yassin massacre is also mentioned in Syrkin, pp. 192-193.

places in Palestine. These crimes are often presented by the Zionists as legitimate military operations against an armed enemy. Describing such an "operation," in the Arab town of Yehudiyeh near Jaffa, the Irgun commander said: "For three days from 11th to 13th December [1947], our units hammered at concentrations of rioters and their offensive bases... We penetrated Yehudiyeh and dealt peremptorily with an armed band that had established its base in the village. Enemy casualties in killed and wounded were very heavy."[173]

What actually happened was that an Irgun pickup truck raced through the village and discharged a barrel full of explosives as it passed the village's schoolyard. The children were out in the yard for a recess between classes. The barrel exploded and killed a large number of them. At that time, I was a high school student in Jaffa. I went to the Government Hospital, which was a few blocks away from my dormitory, and I saw six of the "enemy casualties" that Begin mentions. They were all horribly mutilated. Their average age was eight or ten years!

The Deir Yassin and the Yehudiyeh episodes are mentioned to illustrate the quality of "Jewish valor" in Palestine. As to its extent, they are only two items of a long list of atrocities which led one of the most noted historians alive to write that Jewish crimes against the Arabs of Palestine are comparable to Nazi crimes against the Jews of Europe. He wrote:

> The Jews' immediate reaction to their own experience [with Hitler's crimes] was to

---

[173] Begin, pp.337-338.

become persecutors in their turn for the first time since 135 A.D. — and this at the first opportunity that had arisen for them to inflict on other human beings, who had done the Jews no injury, but happened to be weaker than they were, some of the wrongs that had been inflicted on the Jews by their many successive Western Gentile persecutors during the intervening seventeen centuries... In A.D. 1948 the Jews knew, from personal experience, what they were doing; and it was their supreme tragedy that the lesson learnt by them from their encounter with Nazi Germany Gentiles should have been not to eschew but to imitate some of the evil deeds that the Nazis had committed against the Jews.[174]

What motivated Palestine's Jews to repay the Arabs, who gave them shelter in their country when they were rejected practically everywhere else, with deeds which were described as "the most perverse of all the base propensities of human nature?"[175] There undoubtedly were a few among them who relished to play the role of terrorist, for a change, instead of the terrorized. But such could not have accounted for more than a rare exception. The motive was political.

The Zionists' claim for a Jewish state was based on the contention that since the Jews could not live in peace and security among the Gentiles, they must have a Jewish state which can serve as an ever-ready shelter for

---

[174] Arnold Toynbee, *A Study of History*. (London: Oxford University Press, 1954), Vol. VIII, pp. 289-290.
[175] *Ibid.*, p. 291.

persecuted Jews. The only way the Jewish state could serve this function was to have sufficient territory in which newcomers could be accommodated. But Palestine was "full of Arabs." Even the part of the country allocated to the Jewish state by the United Nations had almost as many Arabs as Jews within its proposed boundaries.[176] The only way to make room for the "exiles" which the Zionists proposed to rescue from the Gentiles was to push the Arabs out of as much territory as possible. The terrorist campaign against the Arabs of Palestine was calculated to achieve that purpose, which it did.

Although Menachem Begin, the commander of the Irgun Zvai Leume terrorists who were guilty of the Deir Yassin massacre, contends that Arab propaganda exaggerated the extent of the massacre, he notes that it was helpful in clearing the Arab population out of Palestine. "Kolonia village," he wrote, "which had previously repulsed every attack of the Haganah, was evacuated overnight and fell without even fighting." Similar things happened in other places.[177]

The Jewish campaign of terror against Palestine Arabs was, after Deir Yassin, beginning to pay dividends. To spare their families the fate of Deir Yassin's victims, the Arab population in threatened areas began to leave their villages and go where they could find some protection. By the time this strange war was over, only a few thousand Arabs remain out of about half a million in Jewish

---

[176] The "Jewish state" had 497,000 Arabs and 498,000 Jews among its population at the time the resolution was passed by the General Assembly. Hadawi, p. 21.

[177] Begin, pp. 164-165.

occupied territory. The Jewish state had thus secured vacancies for the Jews it sought to "ingather" from the four corners of the world. And the rightful owners of the land became a nation of refugees.

The Arabs of Palestine who fled their homes to save their lives are supposed to have lost their right to their land by leaving it during hostilities. The Zionists have spread the myth that the Arabs of Palestine left their homes because they were told to do so by the neighboring Arab states who wanted to clear the way for their planned invasion of Israel.[178] But what could the Zionists tell the world? What could they tell their friends who supported them politically and kept their arsenals replenished? Some of their supporters were well-meaning, incredibly misinformed people who really believed that they were doing humanity a service by supporting unfortunate Jews to live in peace in a home of their own. Could the Zionists tell their friends that their support and their money were being used to murder and rob a people who have never done the Jews any wrong? Of course not.

The Arabs of Palestine have been besmirched by the Zionists by saying that the Arabs just "folded their tents" and left their land, and can the Jews be blamed for walking in and taking over vacated property? The truth of the matter is that the Arabs of Palestine defended their homes, even with rusted rifles, until the Jews with their terrorism pulled the fight down to a level for which the

---

[178] Begin, p. 50. This same writer does not seem to be quite sure as to who told the Arabs of Palestine to leave their homes. In another reference to this same subject, he says it was "the British authorities" who t(old them to do so! *Ibid.*, p. 179.

Arabs were neither morally nor emotionally equipped. Until this happened, the Arabs had successfully checked the Zionist onslaught.

Lieutenant Colonel Netanel Lorch, a participant in the war on the Jewish side who later became the first Chief of the Military History Division of the Israeli General Staff, wrote that at the end of March 1948 the Arabs of Palestine had the upper hand in the war, and that it was only months later, i.e. after the Deir Yassin massacre, that the tables turned.[179] He further stated that at the end of March "The first round had ended with considerable Arab success."[180] And he enumerates as signs of this success "The isolation of the Negev, of Jerusalem, and of parts of western Galilee from the centers of the Yishuv [Palestine's Jews]; the loss in one week of dozens of armoured cars produced by the strenuous effort of months; the casualties incurred in the battle of the roads; the defeat that outweighed the victories..."[181]

No, the Arabs of Palestine did not just fold their tents and leave. Even after the Deir Yassin massacre, larger Arab towns which had a better chance of resisting Zionist terror made the Zionists pay dearly for the land and the homes which they were seeking for future Jewish occupants. To capture Safad, a town of about 12,000 people located in northern Palestine, which they accomplished on May 10, 1948, the Jews had to fight its inhabitants "from room to room and from house to

---

[179] Netanel Lorch, *The Edge of the Sword*. (New York: G. P. Putnam's Sons, 1961), p. 73.
[180] *Ibid.*, p. 75.
[181] *Ibid.*, p. 74.

111

house."[182] But the Arabs of Palestine, with their rusted rifles and a promise of future help from the sister Arab states, could not resist for long.

The Jewish forces, "the most powerful military force in the Middle East,"[183] backed by the material support of world Jewry, and made effective by a remarkable absence of moral restraint, finally "turned the tables" and before the neighboring Arab states came to the aid of Palestine on May 15, 1948, they had managed not only to drive the Arab population out of the territory which the United Nations had allocated to the Jewish state, but also to expand that territory considerably.

* * *

It was said that the eviction of the Arab people from areas allocated to the Jewish state by the United Nations was a part of a plan to make room for expected Jewish newcomers. But what about the expansion *beyond* the proposed borders of the Jewish state? Was that expansion premeditated or was it the unplanned result of a chaotic situation? Information made public long after the fact shows that the would-be Jewish state, before it came into being, *planned* to expand the area which was allocated to it by the General Assembly's resolution at the expense of neighboring territory allocated to an Arab state by the same resolution. Even if one is to disregard the dissident factions who refused and still refused to settle for less than all of Palestine and Trans-Jordan, it remains true that the official organ of Palestine's Jewish community, which

---

[182] *Ibid.,* p. 105.
[183] Crossman, *Palestine Mission,* pp. 157-158.

later became the government of Israel, had *planned and carried out territorial expansion by the use of force.*

Two months before the termination of the British mandate over Palestine and before the intervention of the Arab states, the Haganah, which later became the Israeli army, prepared an operational plan "D" outlining its military objectives. According to the plan, "The mission of the Haganah was as simple as it was revolutionary: 'to gain control of the area allotted to the Jewish state [by the United Nations partition resolution] and defend its borders *and* those of the blocs of Jewish settlements and such Jewish population as were outside those borders...'"[184]

In other words, the task of the Haganah was not merely to secure and defend the area allocated to the Jewish population, but also to extend their control to areas within the territory allocated to the Arab state. Moreover, the operational objectives of the plan included "insuring freedom of communications for military and economic purposes inside the area of the Jewish state and *between it and the centers of Jewish population outside by containing control of the major arteries of the country...* [and by] *depriving the enemy the use of forward bases by their capture.*"[185]

Again, the Haganah's task involved the extension of its control to areas earmarked for the proposed Arab state. This expansion was to include the following areas allocated to the Arabs: (1) areas where there were Jewish settlements. (2) the corridors connecting these settlements

---

[184] Lorch, p. 87.
[185] *Ibid.* Italics added.

with the area of the proposed Jewish state. And (3) Arab territory bordering on the "Jewish state." When it is remembered that Arab and Jewish settlements and towns were interlaced over most of the country, it becomes clear that the Haganah's objective of bringing all Jewish settlements under their control amounted to considerable territorial encroachment upon Arab territory.

In accordance with this plan, unit commanders were instructed to prepare and to execute the objectives which it outlined. Due to the fact that the Israelis and their supporters claimed at the time and still claimed today, that the Jews of Palestine were fighting in self-defense against the hordes of Arab invaders, it must be repeated that *extension* of Jewish-controlled territory was taking place *before* the British completed their evacuation of Palestine, *before* the state of Israel was proclaimed, and *before* the neighboring Arab states moved a muscle in defense of the Arabs of Palestine.

The Haganah's plans and actions are adequate proof that it was not a war of self- defense that was being waged against the Arab of Palestine. If more proof is needed that the future state of Israel was engaged in a war of expansion even before its proclamation on May 15, 1948, more proof is readily available.

In an action which paralleled the Haganah's plan "D", the Zionist General Council adopted a motion, proposed by Ben Gurion, on April 6, 1948, which resolved: "Not to restrict ourselves to defense tactics but to attack, at the right time, all along the front, and *not only in the territory designated for the Jewish State, not only within the borders of Palestine, but to strike at the enemy wherever he is to be found."*[186]

It may be argued, of course, that offensive military operations may be undertaken not as an act of aggression but to ensure a more effective defense. Actually, Jewish authorities implied as much when they sought to hedge against criticism of their expansion by claiming in 1948, the Arab territory which their forces were occupying "would be held only temporarily as long as the need existed."[187] As it turned out, "temporarily as long as the need existed" meant in perpetuity. For they not only continue to hold on to the territory, but they contend that by fleeing their homes in 1948, the Arabs of Palestine had forfeited their rights to them. No one ever argued that civilian populations forfeit their rights to their homes by fleeing the terrors of war; but then the Israelis have a logic of their own.

It is clear that Israel's decision to hold on to, and never to relinquish, Arab territory did not come as an afterthought but was a part of the plan from the outset. Israel never had the slightest intention of occupying Arab land only temporarily as they contended. This is shown by the fact that when Jewish political leaders were preparing a proclamation announcing the establishment of Israel, they refrained from specifying the territory or the borders of the state they were about to announce. Nor was their neglect to specify such borders caused by an oversight. It was debated and deliberately rejected by the

---

[186] Ben Gurion, *Israel: Years of Challenge*, p. 39, Italics added.
[187] Lorch, p.89.

National Administration which served as the provisional government of Israel.[188] The Israelis were not about to let their expansion be handicapped by such a thing as borders. The dissidents, of course, were less hypocritical about what they were doing than "official" forces. Referring to the Irgun's activities *before* the intervention of the Arab states, its commander had said:

> In the months *preceding* the Arab invasion... we continued to make sallies into the Arab area... But it was clear to us that even the most daring sallies carried out by partisan troops would never be able to decide the issue. *Our hope lay in gaining control of territory.*[189]

When *Haaretz*, a Jewish newspaper, observed that these attacks on Arab territory had "changed the situation" the Irgun's commander affirmed: "Of course, it was a radical change. Previously all the Jewish forces — including our units — had been stationed in local defence posts. *But you can only 'be stationed' in defence posts. You cannot conquer in them.*"[190] This "radical change" was taking place in December 1947, or six months before troops from the neighboring Arab states crossed the borders into Palestine. The evidence, therefore, leaves no room for doubt — except in minds blinded by unreasoning emotion — that Palestine's Jews were not engaged in a heroic struggle for self-preservation as their fundraisers

---

[188] Ben Gurion, *Israel: Years of Challenge*, pp. 40-41.
[189] Begin, p. 348. Italics added.
[190] *Ibid.*, p. 338. Italics added.

contended, but in an aggressive war with the deliberate goals of expansion and conquest.

Months later, in the middle of May, 1948, the British Mandate over Palestine came to an end, and troops from the neighboring Arab states were sent to Palestine. The Jews informed to the world that they had been invaded by Arab hordes who sought to strangle the newly-born Jewish state and to drive the Jews into the sea. The Arab states announced, and the Arabs of Palestine were naïve enough to believe, that these troops were sent to defend them and to salvage whatever could be salvaged of Palestine for its Arab inhabitants.

These Arab soldiers operated under five commands, unified in name but in fact separate. Not only did they lack a unified command but even a semblance of coordination. In one instance known to this writer, Egyptian airplanes attacked Jordanian positions near Jerusalem with the mistaken belief that they were teaching the Israelis a lesson!

The misconceptions about the Arab-Israeli war are almost endless. But the least known aspect of the war is perhaps the fact that *Israeli soldiers outnumbered the combined forces of the five Arab states which sent troops to Palestine by about four to one.* [191] The fact that there were only about half a million Jews in Palestine "surrounded by a Sea of Arabs" numbering fifty million people leads to

---

[191] Anthony Nutting, *The Arabs* (New York: The American Library, 1964), p. 330. Also Fred J. Khouri, *The Arab-Israeli Dilemma* (Syracuse, New York: Syracuse University Press, 1968), pp. 70-72. Estimates by other authors ranged from two to one up to six to one.

the *assumption* that Jewish forces were hopelessly outnumbered by Arab forces in Palestine.

Virtually relieved of the task of having to work to eat by contribution from Jewish communities abroad, especially in the United States, the 600,000 Palestinian Jews were able to mobilize every sixth person and thus raise an army of 100,000 strong. Facing this army stood about 25,000 Arab soldiers[192] whose chances of success were impaired by their own governments as much as they were by the enemy. Lack of coordination was their minor problem.

The Iraqi contingent, with which this writer is most familiar since he lived in the part of Palestine which was within its field of operations, actually lacked the necessary authority to fight. The Iraqi soldiers were fairly well trained and equipped. But in many instances the regular Iraqi forces were "deployed" behind the front lines, while the few armed Palestinian Arabs manned the forward positions. Moreover, whenever the Israelis attacked and made advances, the Iraqi troops practically always lacked the authority to counterattack.

"*Maku awamir*," meaning "we have no orders" in the Iraqi dialect, soon became the most notorious and the most hated Arabic expression in Palestine. Occasionally, local Iraqi commanders defied or circumvented the *maku awamir* handicap at the risk of being "disciplined."

One such case took place in the vicinity of the writer's hometown. The Israelis attacked Arab positions northwest of Qalqilya during the first ten-day truce and

---

[192] *Ibid.*

occupied some of them. The local Iraqi commander asked for authority to counterattack and received the expected *maku awamir* response from his superior. Burning with anger, the local commander went to City Hall and proposed to defy his orders if the townspeople would help him. Since he could not use his soldiers, he said, he would counterattack with volunteers. The volunteers retook the lost positions while the army stood by and watched.[193]

With the exception of a few instances of defiance such as this, the Iraqi army hardly saw any action in Palestine. To the soldiers, it was most frustrating. When the Iraqi army received orders to withdraw from Palestine and to hand over the territory under their control to Trans-Jordan's Arab Legion, the local Arab population protested the move. Even if the Iraqi army did not fight, its presence discouraged large-scale Israeli attacks on the area. The Arab Legion, however, was too small a force to act as a deterrent if it were spread over a large area.

The Arab Legion numbered less than 5,000 soldiers at that time, had absolutely no air force, and did not possess a single tank. It was being very effective in the defense of Jerusalem and its environs, but its effectiveness would be undermined if it were to assume the further responsibility of defending the sizeable Iraqi sector. For this reason, the population of the Iraqi sector feared that Iraqi withdrawal would mean the further loss of territory to the Israelis.

---

[193] A year later, Israel got the territory without firing a shot. It was surrendered to it by the Armistice Agreement.

119

In one demonstration against the proposed Iraqi withdrawal this writer listened to the Iraqi commander in Tulkarm address the people in a voice trembling with emotion, saying: "You do not want us to leave. Believe me, I do not want to leave either. When I left Iraq, I told my wife and my friends that I was going to Palestine to defend it against the Zionists. If I go back now, what am I going to say when they ask me 'what have you done in Palestine?' How can I tell them — as I must — that I drilled and drank a lot of tea?"

* * *

The Egyptians, if the pun may be pardoned, had a weighty handicap in the form of their supreme commander, King Farouk the First (and fortunately the last). Egypt's contribution to the war effort consisted of about 10,000 soldiers, the largest among the five Arab forces.[194] There were probably more Egyptian casualties inflicted by their own weapons than by the enemy. They were armed with defective weapons acquired through deals calculated to enrich Farouk's cronies at the expense of the lives of the soldiers in the field. Although the scandal of the defective weapons became public knowledge only years later, when the monarchy was overthrown in 1952, the soldiers in the battlefield were painfully aware of the fact that they were being betrayed. In *The Philosophy of the Revolution*, President Nasser, who

---

[194] There were approximately 8,000 to 10,000 Egyptians, 2,000 to 4,000 Iraqis, 4,000 to 5,000 Jordanians, 3,000 to 4,000 Syrians, 1,000 to 2,000 Lebanese, and token units from Saudi Arabia and Yemen sent to Palestine. Khouri, p. 70.

was at the time with the Egyptian forces in Palestine, wrote of the treachery in this manner:

> I recall a time when I was sitting in the trenches thinking about our problems. Falujah was surrounded, and the enemy was concentrating upon it a formidable air and artillery bombardment. I used often to say to myself: 'Here we are in these foxholes, surrounded, in danger, thrust treacherously into a battle we were not ready for, our lives the playthings of greed, conspiracy, and lust which have left us here weaponless under fire.'[195]

* * *

To the Arabs of Palestine, the manner in which the sister Arab states were "saving" their country was very puzzling. They tried to make sense out of the curious war which they were witnessing. They finally arrived at the conclusion that the Arab states never had the slightest intention of liberating Palestine or retaking areas occupied by Israeli forces, but only wanted to stake claims on the bits and pieces which the Israelis had not yet picked up.

Rumors began to circulate that King Abdullah of Trans-Jordan had reached a tacit agreement with the Israelis to the effect that if they acquiesced in his claim over Arab areas West of the River Jordan, he would acquiesce in their control of the areas they had occupied. The rumors gained credence when the Arab area West of

---

[195] Gamal Abd El-Nasser, *The Philosophy of the Revolution.* (Cairo: Dar Al-Maaref, n.d.), p.13.

121

the River was annexed to Trans-Jordan in 1950. In 1951, King Abdullah was fatally shot by a Palestinian Arab during a visit to Jerusalem. Years later, these rumors which caused King Abdullah to be adjudged a traitor and led to his assassination were confirmed. It became known that, even before the United Nations recommended the partition of Palestine, King Abdullah's only concern — expressed to Golda Myerson in a secret meeting held in Amman — was that a piece of Palestine would be available for him to annex to his kingdom.[196]

Throughout this period, The United Nations, whose partition resolution had made inevitable a war which the Balfour Declaration of 1917 had made possible, was trying to halt the armed conflict without touching upon its cause. It established a Palestine Commission to supervise the implementation of the partition resolution. But things in Palestine were getting out of hand, and all the Commission could do was to send a small liaison group to Jerusalem to observe and to report on what was going on. The Commission was a total failure.

In April 1948, the Security Council approved a resolution calling on the people of Palestine, both Arabs and Jews, to refrain from fighting and created a Truce Commission consisting of the consuls-general of Belgium, France, and the United States in Jerusalem. The resolution went unheeded. A special session of the United Nations was called and met from April 16 to May 14. It appointed a Mediator who was instructed to use his good offices toward Arab-Jewish conciliation and the peaceful

---

[196] Syrkin. Pp. 195-196.

adjustment of the future of the country. Count Folke Bernadotte of Sweden was selected as Mediator. After two abortive appeals by the Security Council, a four-week truce was agreed upon. It was in effect from June 11 to July 9, 1948. After a few more days of fighting, a second truce became effective on July 16 in Jerusalem, and on July 18 in the rest of the country. This second truce remained in effect, though it was periodically punctuated by large scale fighting, until 1949 when it was superseded by the Armistice Agreement.

On September 17th, 1948, the unarmed Mediator and his staff were driving in three cars through Jerusalem. As they passed through the Katamon quarter, they were stopped by an Israeli Jeep which blocked the street. Count Bernadotte and his aides assumed that they were being stopped for the usual checking of passes, but a submachine gun was thrust through the window of the Mediator's car and, in a long burst of fire, Count Bernadotte and Colonel Andre Serot, a senior truce supervisor from France, were shot dead. Dr. Ralph Bunche, a senior member of the United Nations Secretariat became Acting Mediator. Under his chairmanship, negotiations between Arab and Israeli representatives were held on the Island of Rhodes in mid-January 1949. These negotiations resulted in the General Armistice Agreements between Israel on one hand and Egypt, Lebanon, Jordan, and Syria on the other.[197] These

---

[197] Iraq, the fifth Arab state which sent forces to Palestine during the war has never signed an armistice agreement with Israel. For his role as Mediator, Dr. Bunche received the Nobel Peace Prize.

agreements suspended the Arab-Israeli war, and this strange war gave way to an even stranger peace.

CHAPTER 8 - A NATION OF REFUGEES

> The world has done little to give them a faith in humanity.
> —Per-Olow Anderson, *They Are Human Too*

The post-World War II period, although marred by the rise of Russian imperialism in Eastern Europe and by sporadic lapses into neo-colonialism by some of the Western powers, brought the fulfillment of the ideal of self-determination of peoples. One after another the dependent peoples of the earth attained self-government. But the Palestinians were destined to witness this triumph of the anti-colonial revolt from the vantage point of a refugee camp.

The irony of this fact becomes apparent when one remembers that the post World War II era was a period of widespread interest in and deep sympathy for European refugees. It was a period in which a great deal of international effort was being made to alleviate the suffering of these victims of war. But at the same time, a whole nation was being made homeless under the pretext of a humanitarian impulse to do something for others.

As in the case of other aspects of the problem of Palestine, the Zionists and their supporters have created myths about the Palestinian refugees which, through incessant repetition over a period of many decades, have become established in the minds of many people as facts.

Briefly, the myth runs as follows: After the United Nations General Assembly recommended the partition of Palestine, the Arabs launched an attack on the Jewish community in an effort to destroy it and thus prevent the establishment of the Jewish state envisioned by the partition resolution. To facilitate the planned massacre, the Arab states around Palestine issued instruction to the Arabs of Palestine advising them to leave their homes and country and open the way for the forthcoming armed assault on the Jews. "Daily, over the air, came the command of the Arab leaders to their Palestinian brothers to fly to safety until the 'cleansing process' was done, when the Arabs could return to their fields and *to the Jewish fields and cities that would be vacant for them.*"[198] The Jews, the myth-makers continue, "urged upon them to remain quietly in their homes, which would be respected. But the Arab peasants, the Arab sheikhs and judicial and religious readers, listened to the Arabs. This was natural enough. They fled, leaving their tools and their coffee-

---

[198] Waldo Frank *Bridgehead: The Drama of Israel.* (New York: George Braziller, Inc., 1957), p. 75. Crossman, *A Nation Reborn*, p. 114, put it this way: "Hundreds of thousands of Arabs were instructed by their leaders to become temporary refugees, while the Arab armies drove the Jews into the sea." It is interesting to note that one Zionist, who has been a high public official in Israel since its establishment, asserted that "it was the British authorities who urged the Arabs to flee the country in order to return later as victors." Begin, *The Revolt*, p. 179.

Leon Uris, in his novel Exodus, had a different and a more picturesque account of how the Arabs planned to plunder the Jews. He had Arab women carrying sacks and waiting at the outskirts of Jewish villages under attack. *Exodus* (New York, Bantam Books, Inc., 1958), p. 486.

urns behind them. The 'massacre,' they were told, would be finished in a fortnight or at most a month; and they believed it."[199]

It is apparent that this explanation of the origin of the Palestine refugee problem is intended to convey the feeling that the Arab states and they alone bear the moral responsibility for the plight of the refugees. The interest which the Zionists and their friends have in propagating this view, however, goes beyond the desire to escape censure for condemning the people of Palestine to live the life of exiles. Although they are desirous of that, they are even more interested in the implications of this view. If the Arab states are responsible for the Palestinians becoming a nation of refugees, it becomes their moral obligation to find a place for them within their own territory.

The view advanced by the Zionists strengthens Israel's case in the court of public opinion when Israel seeks to justify its refusal to permit the refugees to return to their country, thus making it possible for the millions of Jews which Israel is bent on "ingathering" from the four corners of the earth to inherit the land and homes of the dispossessed Palestinians. It is, therefore, vitally important to establish the fact that the evidence not only does not support the Zionist interpretation of the origin of the refugee problem, but in fact refutes it.

Erskine Childers, a British journalist, conducted a thorough investigation of Zionist charges that Arab leaders encouraged their Palestinian brethren to leave

---

[199] Frank, p. 75.

their country in 1948. His curiosity was aroused by the fact that although he studied "every official Israeli statement about the Arab exodus," he was "struck by the fact that no primary evidence of evacuation orders was ever produced."[200] While in Israel as a guest of the Israeli Foreign Office in 1958, Mr. Childers gave the Israelis the opportunity to substantiate their well-publicized claims that they possessed documentary proof that the Palestinian Arabs left their homes in response to the calls of their own leaders. He asked to be shown some of the evidence which the Israelis said they had. Three years after he asked for the alleged evidence, Childers wrote:

> I asked to be shown the proofs. I was assured that they existed, and was promised them. None had been offered when I left, but I was again assured. I asked to have the material sent to me. I am still waiting. [201]

It is not unreasonable to assume that Israel would not withhold evidence in its favor, if such evidence in fact did exist.

Determined to find evidence which would, once and for all, prove or disprove Israel's allegations, Childers proceeded with his investigation:

> I next decided to test the undocumented charge that the Arab evacuation orders were broadcast by Arab radio—which could be done thoroughly because the BBC monitored

---

[200] Erskine B. Childers, "The Other Exodus," *The Spectator*, May 12, 1961, p. 672.
[201] *Ibid.*

all Middle Eastern broadcasts throughout 1948. The records, and companion ones by a U. S. monitoring unit, can be seen at the British Museum[202]

A study of the records netted the conclusion that "There was not a single order, or appeal, or suggestion about evacuation from Palestine from any Arab radio station, inside or outside Palestine, in 1948."[203] On the contrary, what the records revealed was that "There is_repeated monitored record of Arab appeals, even flat orders, to the civilians of Palestine to stay put" rather than evacuate.[204]

Recalling Abba Eban's statement, made before the U. N. Special Political Committee in 1957, to the effect that the Archbishop of Galilee testified to the truth of the Israeli charge that Arab leaders ordered their Palestinian brethren to flee, Childers wrote to the Archbishop and asked him to present his evidence.

> I wrote His Grace, asking for his evidence of such orders. I hold signed letters from him, with permission to publish, in which he has categorically denied ever alleging Arab evacuation orders; he states no such orders were ever given. He says that his name has been abused for years, and that the Arabs fled through panic and forcible eviction by Jewish troops.[205]

---

[202] *Ibid.*
[203] *Ibid.*
[204] *Ibid.*
[205] *Ibid.*

Mr. Childers' conclusion, the only conclusion which can be honestly derived from the mass of available evidence, was as follows: "The fact is that Israel's official charges, which have vitally influenced Western thought about the refugees, are demonstrably and totally hollow."[206]

A group of Israeli citizens, unable to live with their government's continued attempts to evade responsibility for the tragedy of the refugees, wrote in a document which they addressed to the United Nations Special Political Committee and Commission on Human Rights in 1961:

> For more than 13 years hundreds of thousands of Palestine Arabs, men, women and children, are wasting their lives in exile and misery, in refugee camps, while their lands have been confiscated, their houses and other property destroyed or wasted or given away for nothing.
>
> It is not true that the Palestine Arabs left their country willingly or because of incitement. Hundreds of thousands of men, especially peasants, do not abandon their homes, and lands by their own will or thanks to propaganda.[207]

How did the Zionist interpretation of the origin of the refugee problem become so very widely accepted in

---

[206] Ibid.

[207] The Central Committee of "The Third Force" Movement in Israel, *A Voice From Israel Demanding 'Justice For The Arabs,'* reprinted by American Friends of the Middle East, Inc., Washington, D.C., November 21, 1961, p. 2.

spite of the fact that it was contradictory to the truth? The answer is very simple. The Zionists and their supporters, by quoting one another, made the unfounded assertion that the Palestinians left their country because the Arab states told them to do so the most widely disseminated explanation of the origin of the Palestine refugee problem. By sheer repetition of the same fiction by many writers over a period of many years, in books, magazines, and newspapers, over the air waves and by speakers, they managed to create, literally out of nothing, what appeared to be evidence. In fact, the myth has become so firmly established in the public mind that, now, the disseminators of the myth need not bother to cite the source of their information. As one of them put it, why and how the refugees left their homes "can be disputed by no honest man."[208]

The Arabs, who have not yet invented the very vital art of public relations, facilitated the Zionists' task by failing to acquaint the world with the facts of the matter. As was mentioned earlier, it was a British writer who punctured the myth by challenging the Israelis to produce the non-existent evidence to support their assertions.

Why *did* nearly a million Palestinians leave their homes, often leaving behind them not only "their tools and their coffee-urns" but even their clothing and bank deposits? They did so for the same reason which impelled countless civilians in Europe to flee their homes before the advancing German army. They fled as civilians have always done in similar circumstances. All wars have

---

[208] Frank, p. 74.

produced refugees, and the Palestine war was no different from other wars in this respect, and the reaction of the Palestinians was no different from the reaction of other civilians in other places during other wars.

However, there were two ways in which the creation of a refugee problem as a consequence of the Palestine war of 1948 distinguished it from other recent wars. First, a larger proportion of the total population were displaced than has been the case in other wars. More than half of the Arab people of Palestine were displaced as a result of the war.

Two factors were responsible for this unusually high proportion of displaced persons. One was the availability of neighboring territory in which the threatened civilians knew they could find a refuge. The fact that four Arab states bordered Palestine, and the fact that the Palestinians had every reason to feel that they would not be turned back at the borders if they sought temporary refuge in their neighbors' lands diminished the possibility of their staying put from a feeling that they were trapped and had no place to go.

The second fact which helps explain the unusually high proportion of displaced persons is that, unlike in the case of other wars, the war in Palestine was deliberately intended to produce that result. In other wars, the conqueror aimed at the occupation and the subjugation of the land and its people. In the case of Zionist conquest of Palestine, the aim was beyond doubt the occupation of the land and the *displacement or expulsion* of its people.

The Zionists did not come to Palestine to rule over Arab subjects. They came to Palestine with the explicit purpose of fulfilling Theodor Herzl's dream of finding a territory into which the Jews "in exile" could be "ingathered." Obviously, not many Jews could be "ingathered" into a country which had 120 Arabs per square mile. The establishment of the *Jewish* state which Herzl envisioned late in the nineteenth century, was to be "as Jewish as France is French and as England is English."[209] Such a state was strictly for the Chosen. The indigenous Arab inhabitants of the land had no place in this scheme, not even as a conquered people. That was why, in 1948, the Zionists "used both military force and psychological warfare to compel as many Arabs as possible to leave their homes."[210]

The "military force and psychological warfare" used by the Zionists in Palestine to affect the expulsion of the Arab people can be better understood if replaced by the simpler synonym "terrorism." As was stated in the previous chapter, the Zionists' resort to terrorism was not dictated by military necessity but primarily by the desire to create among the Palestinian Arabs the feeling that they should expect the worst from their conquerors. A Zionist leader who later became Deputy Prime Minister of Israel illustrated one of the methods used to frighten the civilian Arab population into fleeing their homes. In order "to clean the inner Galilee and to create a Jewish territorial continuity in the entire area of the upper Galilee," he wrote,

---

[209] This widely publicized remark was made by Moshe Dayan in a press conference during a visit to the United States after the June 1967 war. Weizmann, *Trial and Error.*
[210] Khouri, p. 124.

I gathered all of the Jewish Mukhtars, who have contact with the Arabs in different villages, and asked them to whisper in the ears of the Arabs that a great Jewish reinforcement has arrived in Galilee and that it is going to burn all of the villages of the Huleh. They should suggest to these Arabs, as their friends, to escape while there is still time. And the rumour spread in all the areas of the Huleh that it is time to flee. The flight numbered *myriads*. The tactic reached its goal completely...[211]

The fact that indiscriminate terrorism against the civilian population had been in fact used against the Palestinians made such threats of further terrorism credible, and consequently effective in producing the desired exodus.

Count Folke Bernadotte, the Swedish United Nations Mediator in Palestine, reported to the international organization that "The exodus resulted from the panic created by the fighting in their communities, by rumors concerning real and alleged acts of terrorism, or expulsion."[212] The Mediator, who himself fell victim to Jewish terrorism when he was assassinated in Jerusalem shortly after he made this report, continued to report "Large-scale looting, pillaging and plundering and of instances of destruction of villages without military necessity."[213] As a consequence, a few months after war erupted in Palestine, "almost the whole of the Arab

---

[211] Quoted in George J. Tomeh, "Challenge and Response: A Judgment of History," *The Arab World*, vol. XV, no. 5, May 1969, p. 13.
[212] Khouri, p. 125.
[213] *Ibid.*

population [had] fled or [been] expelled from the area under Jewish occupation."[214]

Not all the Palestinians who became refugees were people who fled to escape Jewish terrorism. Most of them were people who dared to stay or did not have the means to go and were subsequently expelled after the Jewish forces occupied their areas.[215] This is evident from the Mediator's statements quoted above. "From the Lydda-Ramleh section alone," for example, "some 60,000 Arabs were ordered by the Israelis to leave on such short notice that they were able to take few if any possessions"[216] with them.

The expansion of territory under Zionist control and the expulsion of more Palestinians, as United Nations officials reported, even continued during the Security Council-ordered truce in 1948.[217] It continued after the signing of the permanent Armistice Agreements and the cessation of hostilities in 1949.[218] In fact, the expropriation and the expulsion of Palestinian Arabs never ceased. United Nations observers in Palestine repeatedly reported harassment, expropriation, and expulsion of Palestinian Arabs who stayed in Israeli-held territory. In fact, the friction and armed clashes which continued to take place between Israel and the surrounding Arab states was partly caused by continued Israeli expropriation of Arab

---

[214] *Ibid.,* p. 124.
[215] Anthony Nutting, *The Arabs.* (New York: The New American Library, 1964), p. 331.
[216] Khouri, p. 124.
[217] *Ibid.*
[218] *Ibid.,* p. 125. Also Nutting, p. 331.

lands in Israel. For example, in 1950, the Israeli authorities expelled the 3,500 Arab inhabitants of El Auja and expropriated their property.[219] Similar action was taken against many Arab inhabitants in northeastern Palestine.[220]

No proof of the argument made here, that an integral part of the Zionist design to conquer Palestine is the expropriation and the expulsion of the Arab people, is more conclusive than the fact that the Israeli authorities not only confiscated the property of the refugees who left or were made to leave their homes during the war but also continue to dispossess the Arabs who stayed in Israel and never left their lands. The following are some of the methods used to dispossess the Arabs in Israel.

In 1950, the Israeli legislature passed "The Absentee's Property Law" according to which

> the land and all other property of absentees was confiscated, and declared as 'absentee' not only those who left Israel, but also everybody who during the Arab-Israeli war 'left his place of residence and went (for any duration of time whatever, even for days or hours) to another place which was at that time held by forces that tried to hinder the establishment of the State of Israel.[221]

What this amounts to is that

---

[219] Burns, p. 93.
[220] Von Horn, pp. 127-128.
[221] The Third Force Movement, p. 6.

an Arab who at the time of military operation near his village sought refuge for a day or hours in another near-by village which was still in Arab hands, became an "absentee" though he was since long already back in his village, and all his property was confiscated, and he became a "refugee." This was a second class of "made-in-Israel" refugee, this time not by unruly, but well-formulated, legal robbery. There are at present about 30,000 such "Israeli refugees." They are landless, homeless and the life conditions of most of them are utterly miserable.[222]

But, as it was said earlier, Israel was to be only for the Chosen. Therefore, it was not enough to expropriate lands of those who committed the sin of seeking refuge from the dangers of war. There were many who stayed put and never did leave their homes and farms. Ways and means had to be devised and were devised to confiscate their lands also.

So, other methods to dispossess the Arabs who stayed in Israel were found, and one of them works as follows: The Arabs in Israel are placed under military government. An Arab cannot travel without a permit from the Israeli military governor. If the land of an Arab farmer is desired, and he refuses to sell, "the Governor will see to it that the required land be sold and at a 'reasonable' price. The recalcitrant villager will get no

---

[222] *Ibid.*

permit to go to town to sell his products."[223] Through this type of pressure, he is forced to "sell" his land.

Another method used to dispossess the remnants of Palestine's Arabs who never left their land operates through two laws which, used together, enable the Israeli authorities to "legally" expropriate any Arab property in Israel. One of these two laws, the Emergency Regulations law of 1948, authorizes the Israeli Minister of Defense

> to proclaim any area as a "Security Zone" the entrance to which is forbidden to any civilian without a special permit. On the other hand, "The Cultivation of Wastelands Ordinance" authorizes the Government to take over land which is not cultivated, i.e. wasted. Thus if Arab land is needed for Jewish settlement the necessary area is declared to be a "Security Zone" and the Arab cultivators are not permitted to enter it. The land, then, is not cultivated, "wasted," and the government takes it over and gives it to Jewish settlers who are permitted to enter it and cultivate it. By this ingenious legal stratagem, a double play of two laws, tens of thousands of dunums of Arab land were taken away from Arab peasants. Not only all the land of the Arab refugees, but also about 1,250,000 dunums, more than 60% of the land of the Israeli-Arabs, who never left Israel, has been confiscated. And the grab is still proceeding.[224]

---

[223] *Ibid.*, p. 5.

[224] *Ibid.*, pp. 6-7. For another account of how Israel "legally" expropriated the property of Arabs in Israel, See Don Peretz, "The

One result of this "legal" expropriation of Arab property is that many Arab farmers in Israel now live by renting their own land from the Israeli government![225]

The fact that Israel has consistently demonstrated remarkable ability for expropriating Arab property led Lieutenant-General Burns, the Canadian Chief of Staff of the United Nations Truce Supervision Organization in Palestine (UNTSOP) to record the following thoughts in a book published after his retirement from that position. As a consequence of the British-French-Israeli attack on Egypt in October, 1956, The Israelis occupied the Gaza Strip, in which a large number of Palestinian refugees had been living since their expulsion in 1948.

At the beginning of November, it seemed to me that as the result of the attack an opportunity had been created for solving an important part of the Palestine problem. The essence of that problem was the demand of the refugees to be allowed to return to their homes in what had now become Israel. A considerable part of them, some 210,000, were enclosed within the narrow confines of the Gaza Strip. The United Nations might have said to the Israelis: "You have captured the Strip and its population, including the refugees. Very well, keep the Strip and its population, but you must also settle the refugees that you have taken with the

---

Arab Minority of Israel," *The Middle East Journal*, vol. 8, no. 2 (Spring, 1954), pp. 139-154. For a discussion of the amount of property involved, see Don Peretz, "Problems of Arab Refugee Compensation," *The Middle East Journal*, vol. 8, no. 4 (Autumn, 1954), pp. 403-416.
[225] Peretz, "The Arab Minority of Israel," p. 144.

Strip, and whom you drove from their homes eight years ago."[226]

Then Burns continued:

The greatest difficulty in such a solution would have been to ensure that the Israelis would keep any agreements they might have made toward the refugees and other Arab inhabitants. Until they finally evacuated the Strip, in March 1957, they put about the impression that they would be prepared to absorb this population as the price of peace. *But Israelis have a record of getting rid of Arabs whose land they desired*: the inhabitants of Majdal; the Azazme tribe from El Auja demilitarized zone; and the Baggara-Ghranname villagers from the demilitarized zone of the Syrian border. I have been credibly informed that what the Israeli authorities really had in mind, if they had been able to keep the Strip, was to absorb only 80,000 of the Strip's population The remainder would have been persuaded to settle elsewhere, perhaps in the Sinai Desert. That this is not a slander on the Israeli Defense Forces is, unfortunately, only too well attested to by three separate incidents in which they took severe repressive measures against Arab civilians, killing large numbers of them.[227]

Lieutenant-General Burns' examples of Israel's disregard of Arab right and Arab life are all drawn from

---

[226] Burns, Between Arab and Israeli, p. 191.
[227] *Ibid*. (Italics added).

his own personal observations during his tenure as Chief of Staff of UNESOP. But his examples can be multiplied. In fact, in its simple but telling way, Lieutenant-General Burns' remark that "Israelis have a record of getting rid of Arabs whose land they desired" contains the essence of the tragic story called the problem of Palestine.

No one who is not blindly committed to the too often held proposition that the Jewish ex-victims of persecution can do no wrong will fail to see the measure of injustice done to the Palestinian people. In view of the evidence available, it is difficult to believe how Israel has managed to gain acceptance of its view that the Arabs of Palestine voluntarily deserted their homes and lands in spite of Israeli pleas that they remain in Palestine.

Israel's desire to make Palestine as Jewish as England is English by expelling its Arab inhabitants has also led Israel to generally mistreat the country's Arab population with the hope that they would find life in Israel so intolerable that they would forsake the land of their ancestors and join their brethren in exile.

A sympathetic friend of Israel, after repeating the usual platitudes that the Arabs in Israel have prospered economically and that they cannot complain about deprivation of political and civil rights continued, only to refute his own assertions. "Officially," he said, "the only important discrimination employed against them is the severe control and limitation of their movements."[228] The Arabs are made to feel alien in their own country, and how could it be otherwise, the same writer asked, when

---

[228] Crossman, *A Nation Reborn*, p. 114.

"in order to achieve higher education or social advancement, they must not only learn Hebrew but betray their national heritage by accepting the Jewish way of life? To grow up an Arab, an ambitious boy must remain a villager in Israel or escape across the frontier to Beirut or Cairo University."[229]

The Zionists have always held the view and still maintain that the inability of the Jews to live as Jews in Christian countries constituted cultural genocide, and yet the first chance they had to behave as those whom they accused, they took the opportunity. Of course, the severe restrictions in the movement of Israeli-Arabs have always been justified on the ground that the Arabs in Israel constituted a "fifth column" inside Israel. But need we repeat that that was Hitler's justification of Jewish persecution in Nazi Germany? Moreover, if Israel treats its Arab inhabitants in such a way that "it would be silly to pretend that the Arabs of Israel feel themselves equal citizens of this Jewish State," is it strange to find that "if the Syrians or Jordanians marched into Galilee, they would be received as liberators by virtually the whole Arab population"[230] of Israel?

Furthermore, it is not true that concern for its security is the only motive for Israel's restrictions on the Arab population, though it is reasonable to concede it as one motive. The manner in which the restrictions on Israel's Arab population operate clearly indicate that one

---

[229] *Ibid.*, p.115.
[230] *Ibid.*, pp. 114-115.

motive is the desire to harass the Arabs by making it simply too difficult for them to continue to live in Israel.

The spokesmen of "The Third Movement in Israel," in the document cited earlier, stated in 1960,

> Israel's leaders declare that the military rule over the Israeli Arabs was established—in 1948—for security reasons, and that these reasons are still valid, because the Arab states are threatening Israel with war, and the Arab villages are situated near Israel's borders. But these declarations are completely untrue.

> The military rule over the Arabs in Israel was neither established in 1948 nor does it continue to exist in 1961 because of the vicinity of the Arab villages to the borders. An Arab must get a permit even in order to go farther from the border. He must get a permit even in order to go to a Jewish settlement. Neither may a Jew enter an Arab village without a written permit from the Governor.[231]

No fair-minded person who knows that "Arab children died in the arms of their mothers while awaiting in the corridor of the Governor for a permit to go to see a doctor"[232] in Israel can continue to believe in Israel's justification for the mistreatment of Palestine's Arabs.

The supreme tragedy of Zionism stems from the fact that in its effort to alleviate the suffering of the Jewish people it helped to suffocate their traditional humanitarianism. In its effort to end their persecution, it

---

[231] The Third Force Movement, p. 5.

[232] *Ibid.*, p. 4.

turned them into persecutors. Not only that, but the persecutors of a people who, unlike many of the peoples of the earth, have never been known as persecutors of the Jews The pogroms, the ghettos, the concentration camps, the gas chambers, the mass executions, and the "No Jews allowed" signs are European inventions and have never been indulged in by today's victims of the "restorers of Israel."

The Zionists, the self-appointed redeemers of the Jewish people, must have known that their own people's traditional abhorrence of unprovoked injustice might keep them from following the leadership of the Zionists in their planned assault on the Arab people of Palestine. So, they deceived them, and millions of other people, into believing that the creation of a Jewish state in Palestine would not only end the suffering of the Jews of Europe, but would also be of incalculable benefit to the backward Arabs. Many well-intentioned people throughout the world were dazzled by the potentialities of a reborn, free, advanced Israel, radiating civilization and prosperity throughout the dark recesses of the Middle East. Until this day, many people still feel it is a pity that Arab rulers are preventing this bright hope emanating from Israel from brightening the lives of the Arab masses.

Such assertions, of course, were also made prior to Israel's establishment. Since the promulgation of the Balfour Declaration the Arabs have been counseled to welcome Jewish immigrants from Europe, who were presumably bringing with them capital and technology to make Palestine a better place in which both Arab and Jew could find a better life. What the well-meaning counsellors forgot or did not know was that the Palestinian Arabs had no place in the Zionist plans for a better future. The Palestinians themselves did not have to wait until the establishment of the state of Israel to discover this fact.

Even during the period of British Mandate, "although the Zionists were claiming to bring great material benefits to the Arabs, the Zionists not only excluded Arabs from their farm lands 'forever,' but Zionist industries frowned on the hiring of Arab workers."[233] When Zionist organizations acquired land, by purchase or violence[234] and leased the land to Jewish settlers "a clause was inserted in the contract between the Zionist institution, the new landlord, and the fresh tenants, the Kibbutz, that no Arab should be allowed to work on this land, neither as a sub-tenant nor as a daily labourer."[235]

The Zionist slogan was "On Jewish land and in Jewish enterprises only Jews shall be employed."[236] When Jewish landowners did hire Arab workers, they were picketed, called "traitors to Zionism and the Jewish nation" until they fired their Arab workers and replaced them by Jews.[237] When an Arab farmer ignored the Zionist slogan that "Jews must buy only Jewish products" and took his produce to Tel-Aviv to sell it, he "was surrounded by Zionist zealots who overturned his cart

---

[233] Khouri, p. 23.
[234] The Third Force Movement, p. 2.
[235] *Ibid.*, pp. 2-3.
[236] *Ibid.*, p.3.
[237] *Ibid.*

and trod with their feet upon his vegetables, while a gathering mob looked sympathetically at the national action. The Jewish policemen hurried away, in order to see nothing."[238]

This brief account of Zionist attack on the security of the Arabs of Palestine before, during, and after the Arab-Israeli war of 1948 is not intended to catalog the grievances of Palestine's Arabs against the latest conquerors of Palestine. It is intended to demonstrate a fact which seemed to have generally escaped the commentators on the Palestine refugees. And this fact is that the people who are generally labeled as the Palestine refugees, even in this discussion, are not refugees in the proper sense of the word. They are *expellees* who, not being of the Chosen, were condemned to live in exile away from the "earth which is soaked with their and their fathers' sweat and blood."[239]

To ensure the permanence of the expulsion of the Palestinians from their country, the Zionists sought to obliterate the national identity of the Palestinian people. As it was said in Chapter Four, the problem of Palestine during the inter-war period was presented as if it were a quarrel between the Zionists and the British. The Balfour Declaration itself relegated the Arabs of Palestine, who then constituted more than 90% of the country's population, to the inconsequential status of "the existing non-Jewish communities."[240]

---

[238] *Ibid.*
[239] *Ibid.*, p. 5.
[240] For the text of the Declaration, see Chapter 3.

In Zionist accounts of the history of the Palestine conflict, the indigenous Arab population, the Palestinian people, the people who were most directly involved in and most tragically affected by the conflict are hardly mentioned. The conflict is increasingly portrayed as a struggle between Israel, valiantly fighting for survival, and Nasser's Egypt, bent upon its destruction. In the 1960's it even became fashionable to depict the conflict as if it were a struggle between Israel, upholding Western civilization and interests in the Middle East, and Soviet Russia bent upon their destruction.

As it was said earlier, the Zionists had to present the situation in that light. It would have been impossible for the Zionists to secure the widespread support which they needed in order to succeed, if the people whose support they sought realized that they were being asked to help uproot from Palestine an innocent people who had never done the Jews any wrong. It is to the eternal credit of some of the Jewish people that, in spite of Zionist deception, they never lost sight of the fact that the real issue was the very survival of the Palestinian people and refused and still refuse to be the Zionists' instrument for the destruction of the people of Palestine.

* * *

The emergence of Palestinian commando organizations and the publicity they received since the 1967 war began to familiarize the world with the fact that there is a Palestinian people, a fact which the Zionists

sought to conceal.[241] It is not unreasonable to assume that
the reason why Israel has tended to over-react to the
commando raids,[242] in spite of the fact that so far they
have not had more than a minor effect on its economy or
security, is not what the commandos do but what they
symbolize. They symbolize the fact that the Palestinian
people have not lost their identity as a people in spite of
their demoralizing experience for decades as "Arab
refugees."

It was said earlier in this chapter that although the
1948 war in Palestine was no different from other wars
when it resulted in a refugee problem, the refugee
problem it created was different from the refugee
problems caused by other wars in two ways. One of these
ways was the fact that an abnormally large proportion of
the population of Palestine was displaced. The second
difference, to which we now turn, is that while civilian
populations displaced by war are normally permitted to
return to their homes after the cessation of hostilities, the
Palestinians have been denied the right to return to
Palestine.

As early as December 11, 1948, the United Nations
General Assembly, from which Israel had received its
charter to exist a few months earlier, passed a resolution
[Resolution 194 (III)] calling upon Israel to permit all the
Palestinian war refugees who wished to do so to return to

---

[241] The assassination of Senator Robert Kennedy on the first
anniversary of the 1967 war by Sirhan Sirhan, a Palestinian immigrant
in the United States, also helped bring about this awareness.
[242] For example, the Israeli attack on the civilian Beirut
International Airport.

148

their homes, and to compensate those of them who preferred to stay in their places of refuge.

The United Nations continually renewed this recognition of the Palestinian people's right to return home by re-endorsing its original resolution every year since 1948.[243] Israel refused and continues to refuse to comply with these resolutions. Apparently, the United Nations, now that it was recommending something which Israel found objectionable, ceased to speak for "the organized moral opinion of all peoples"[244] as it did when it passed resolutions favorable to the Zionist cause.

Israel has advanced numerous arguments to justify its refusal to repatriate the refugees. These are some of the most frequently made arguments:

1. The United Nations resolution does not ask Israel to accept back any except refugees who are willing to live in peace with their neighbors.

2. The return of refugees cannot be effected until a formal peace is established between Israel and the Arab states.

3. Due to the influx of Jewish immigrants, there is no room left for the Arab refugees.

As to the argument that the United Nations resolution does not anticipate that Israel accept refugees not willing to live in peace with their neighbors, it is enough to say that Israel has never permitted anyone to ascertain whether or not there were refugees who, at least to end their exile, were willing to live in peace if allowed

---

[243] *G. A. O. R.*, pp. 18-19.
[244] Welles, p. 48.

149

to return to their homes. Israel continually tells the world that it has successfully "integrated" the Palestinians who remained in Palestine. What, then, justifies Israel's assumption that other Palestinians could not live peacefully in Israel?

The specious nature of the second argument, that a peace settlement must precede repatriation, is made clear by the fact that Israel's leaders have also declared their opposition to the return of the refugees even if a peace settlement with the Arab states is reached.[245]

Israel's third argument, that the influx of Jewish immigrants makes it impossible to accept the Palestinian refugees is too transparent to require comment. If there is no room for the legitimate owners of the land, the legitimacy of whose ownership Israel itself admits, how can there be room for hundreds of thousands of newcomers? If Israel's intentions regarding the refugees were honorable, it could at least, as William Zukerman suggested in a *Jewish Newsletter* editorial on December 14, 1959, "admit to Israel one Arab refugee family for every Jewish family which will settle there."

The fact of the matter is that Israeli leaders from the very beginning encouraged large-scale Jewish immigration into Palestine, as Kenneth Bilby of the New York *Herald Tribune* put it, "partly to use them as an 'argument' as to why Israel 'could not allow the Arabs to return.'"[246]

---

[245] Khouri, p.127
[246] *Ibid.*

Long before Israel installed the "no vacancy" signs upon its gates, signs which are turned off when Jewish immigrants arrive, its prime minister, Ben Gurion, "took the position before his cabinet that 'no Arab refugee should be admitted back.'"[247]

In view of these facts, the Israeli argument fails to be convincing. As it was said earlier, the Zionist attitude toward the Palestinian Arabs can be better understood when one keeps in mind the very important fact that the Zionists did not come to Palestine to rule over Arab subjects.

As if not satisfied with the eviction of Palestine's Arabs and their continued refusal to allow them to return to their country, the Zionists have attempted to cast doubt on the attachment of the Palestinians to their country and their desire to return to their homes. They have attempted to create the impression that the refugees are used by Arab leaders for propaganda purposes. "The Arab chiefs," it is said, "have preferred to let their unfortunate brethren rot in the camps of exile, for obvious reasons: their presence fortifies the Arab thesis that the Jews are robbers and usurpers."[248]

The Arab countries, which have been hosting the Palestinian refugees since 1948, have in fact done a great deal to ameliorate their suffering. The willingness of the Arab states to help the refugees and the "energy, intelligence and adaptability of refugees themselves" were given by the Commissioner-General of UNRWA, in

---

[247] *Ibid.*
[248] Frank, pp. 76-77.

151

his *Report* cited above, as the primary reasons for whatever improvement has taken place in the life of the refugees.[249]

If the Arab states are to be blamed for the fate of the refugees, they may be blamed for their failure to prevent the success of the Zionist conquest of Palestine in 1948. But they cannot be justly blamed for refusing to oblige Israel by forcing the Palestinians against their will to go into a neo-Babylonian exile. As the Commissioner-General of UNRWA put it,

> there is the widespread belief that the host Governments have been deliberately and inhumanely keeping the refugees in a state of destitution and dependence on international charity as a weapon in the prosecution of their political aims. This also needs correction. Although the host Governments have opposed mass schemes of direct resettlement, on the grounds that this would be contrary to the interests and expressed wishes of the refugees themselves, their record in promoting the rehabilitation of the refugees as individuals through education, training and employment has been notably humane and helpful. They have extended this aid to the refugees in spite of the grave difficulties which already confronted them in providing a livelihood for their own rapidly expanding populations.[250]

---

[249] *G. A. O. R.*, pp.20-21.
[250] *Ibid.*, p.19.

The refugees themselves have consistently opposed any solution to their predicament which did not envision their return to their homes. As a United Nations agency reported in 1950, the refugees "invariably displayed an extremely emotional and deep-seated desire to return to their homes."[251] Their objection to attempts to deprive them permanently of what they consider to be their God-given right to live in the land of their ancestors has been repeatedly demonstrated by their opposition to schemes designed to settle them outside of Palestine. Thus "the larger the project [i.e. the more permanent it looked and the further away it was from 'Palestine,' the greater was the opposition to it and the fear of accepting it."[252]

And why not? It has been reported that Jewish displaced persons in Europe after World War II refused to work and left their quarters in a filthy state, and in a case in Austria, they "smashed the whole camp to pieces" for fear that they be kept where they were.[253] It has also been reported that the Jews blocked the implementation of a post-World War II humanitarian plan to secure the adoption of Jewish refugees in England and other European countries.[254]

If it is credible that a people who had never seen Palestine be so attached to it, is it difficult to believe that a people who had never known another homeland are attached to it also? Or are they not human too?

---

[251] Khouri, p. 130.
[252] *Ibid.*, p. 137.
[253] Crossman, *Palestine Mission*, p. 77.
[254] *Ibid.*, p.78.

Writing in 1938, George Antonius, a Palestinian Arab, said that the responsibility to alleviate the suffering of European Jews was not the Arab's alone, but the responsibility of humanity.

> To place the brunt of the burden upon Arab Palestine is a miserable evasion of the duty that lies upon the whole of the civilized world...No code of morals can justify the persecution of one people in an attempt to relieve the persecution of another. The cure for the eviction of the Jews from Germany is not to be sought in the eviction of the Arabs from their homeland; and the relief of Jewish distress may not be accomplished at the cost of inflicting a corresponding distress upon an innocent and peaceful population.[255]

Little did George Antonius know that this "miserable evasion" is now heralded as the miracle of Israel. As one Jewish writer stated it:

> We came and turned the native Arabs into tragic refugees. And still we dare to slander and malign them, to besmirch their name. Instead of being deeply ashamed of what we did and trying to undo some of the evil we committed... we justify our terrible acts and even attempt to glorify them.[256]

---

[255] Quoted in Nutting, p. 331.
[256] Statement from Nathan Chofshi, quoted in Childers, p. 675.

CHAPTER 9 - VIOLENT TRUCE

Count Bernadotte, the United Nations Mediator reported to the General Assembly on September 16, 1948, that the new Jewish state by allowing unrestricted Jewish immigration into the newly-conquered Arab lands would not want "to stay within its defined boundaries" but seek further expansion.[257] Therefore, the circumstances surrounding the birth of Israel intensified the Arabs' resentment of past injustices and their fears of injustices yet to come.

Israel, on the other hand, saw no need to ameliorate Arab grievances or to allay their apprehensions. It insisted on holding on to every inch of territory it conquered, it refused to repatriate the refugees, and it continued to "ingather" Jews wherever they could be persuaded to go to Palestine. Israel saw no need to make it easier for the Arabs to reconcile themselves to their loss by even small symbolic territorial concessions, by repatriating refugees, or by limiting the influx of Jewish immigration which the Arabs believed to be the driving force behind Israeli territorial expansionism.

If Israel truly desired peace with its neighbors, it was presented with such an opportunity when, in May 1949,

---

[257] Report A/648, cited in Khouri, p. 81.

155

the Arab states signed an agreement with Israel to the effect that the Arabs and Israel commit themselves to a peaceful settlement based on the original United Nations partition scheme of 1947. But as soon as Israel secured membership in the United Nations, a few months after it signed the Lausanne Protocol, it wrecked this first serious chance for a peaceful settlement by renouncing the agreement and declaring its unwillingness to modify the status quo as the agreement had stipulated.[258]

In the first year of its existence, Israel had profited from the absence of peace. Its enlarged territory testified to that. And nothing really changed with the coming of the armistice. The two super-powers, Russia and the United States, still competed for Israel's favor. It had the largest and most effective military establishment in the Middle East. It had the financial and political backing of the World Zionist movement. It had the blessings of millions in the Western World who mistook its advent for the fulfillment of God's most cherished dream. And it had the support of the influential liberal intellectuals who, either in emulation of their Soviet mentors or out of a sincere belief that the emergence of Israel would at long last bring progress to the Middle East, gave Israel their unreserved support. Last, but certainly not least, the inability of the Arabs to sufficiently mobilize their considerable human and natural resources in the service of their cause encouraged Israel not to compromise. In short, all the relevant factors seemed to conspire to convince Israel's leaders that there was no need for them

---

[258] Khouri, pp. 293-294.

to even take cognizance of Arab grievances or fears. And thus, to repeat, the least likely thing to happen as the consequence of the first Arab-Israeli war was the restoration of peace to Palestine. Instead, the Holy Land became the scene of a "violent truce"[259] which has persisted ever since.

Instead of seeking peace by lessening the injustices and the fears which precluded it, Israel sought to coerce the Arabs into accepting the inequitable status quo which it created by force of arms. Its policy, from the moment it realized that military superiority was on its side until this day, has been guided by the belief that by a continuous demonstration of its military superiority Israel was, sooner or later, bound to convince the Arabs that they had no choice but to sue for peace on Israel's terms. Once the Arabs were made to realize the hopelessness of their cause they would swallow the status quo hook, line, and sinker. Consequently, Israel saw in the Arabs' refusal to recognize the legitimacy of its forcible seizure of Arab land an opportunity to embark on a policy of intimidation under the guise of self-defense. Guided by the arrogant and dangerous belief that the Arab people responded to "reason" only "when they were held by the throat,"[260] the rulers of Israel adopted a policy which has produced an unending succession of armed clashes along the Armistice Lines in Palestine which twice, in 1956 and in 1967, took

---

[259] After the title of a book dealing with the operation of the Arab-Israeli Armistice Agreements of 1969 by Commander E. H. Hutchison, U.S.N.R., (New York: The Devin-Adair Company, 1956).

[260] Moshe Brilliant, "Israel's Policy of Reprisals," *Harper's Magazine*, March, 1955, p.69.

the form of full-scale invasions of neighboring Arab territory.

Let us begin with a statement of the most widely known and accepted version of the story which, needless to say, is the Israeli version. According to the Israeli story, picked up and repeated times without number by Zionist sympathizers and supporters throughout the world, the defeat of the Arabs in the first Arab-Israeli war in 1947-1949 left the Arabs highly frustrated and embittered. But they never abandoned the intention to seek every opportunity to make the life of Israel insecure and to ultimately throw the Jews into the sea. Since they lacked the ability to achieve their ultimate goal of destroying Israel, they resorted to the use of infiltrators and marauders who were sent into Israel to destroy, murder, and steal. In self-defense Israel sought to put an end to these criminal acts by retaliating against the Arabs. These reprisals, intended to teach the Arabs that resort to force was not profitable, kept the borders in a state of constant turmoil and twice led to large-scale fighting which eventually led to the 1967 Arab-Israeli war. As a result of this Arab-initiated folly, peace is more remote than ever before.

When a retired U. S. Navy Commander was called upon to serve as a Military Observer attached to the United Nations Truce Supervision Organization (UNTSO) in Palestine, in 1951, he sought to inform himself of the situation before his departure to the Holy Land. His inquiries, naturally, produced this widely disseminated Israeli version of the story. He later wrote,

According to my informants there had been a short war between the Arabs and Zionists in 1948, after which an armistice had been signed as the first step toward peace. Now the land was divided between the State of Israel and the Arabs. The new Zionist State, Israel, wanted peace, but the Arabs would not agree to it. The Israelis were staunchly protecting their new national home against the ever increasing bitterness of the Arabs.[261]

As the following pages will show, this view, which not only seeks to absolve Israel of the responsibility for the breakdown of the Armistice Agreements but also implies that the Arabs have no valid grievances against the *fait accompli* which Israel wishes to ram down the Arabs' throats, highly distorts the realities of Arab-Israeli relations. To anticipate the discussion which is to follow, this Israeli view, which Commander Hutchison correctly characterized as "a one-sided picture parroted from the average editorial on the Middle East,"[262] differs so greatly from the true state of affairs that, after serving for three years in Palestine as an on-the-spot official U. N. observer, Hutchison, who according to his own admission began with a "pro-Israel" position,[263] finally reversed his stand and reached the conclusion that "Israel is emerging in a true light as the 'Aggressor in the Middle East.'"[264] Nor was Hutchison's experience unique.

---

[261] Hutchison, pp. 4-5.
[262] *Ibid.*, p. 5.
[263] *Ibid.*, p. 6.
[264] *Ibid.*, p. 133.

As Major General Carl von Horn, the Swedish Chief of Staff of UNTSO, later commented on the disillusionment which Israel's behavior tended to create even among its well-wishers: "Never in my life have I encountered a nation with such an infinite talent for turning good will into disillusion and often into disgust. It seemed as though the state were possessed by some daemon with a capacity to turn political friends into enemies."[265]

This "infinite talent" for losing sympathizers among U. N. observers in spite of the fact that, almost to a man they began their tours of duty "with the most positive and sympathetic attitude toward the Israelis and their ambitions for their country,"[266] led the Chief of Staff of UNTSO to ponder the strange phenomenon. He began to question U.N. personnel leaving Palestine upon the conclusion of their assignments there about the most disappointing experiences they had during their service with UNTSO and reported that "the reply was almost invariably: 'The consistent cheating and deception of the Israelis.'"[267]

Why is it that knowledge of Israel, when not "filtered," tends to produce such reactions? What is it that gives Israel this "infinite talent" for turning friends into enemies? These questions can be answered best by reviewing Israel's record as a signatory of the Armistice Agreements of 1949.

---

[265] Von Horn, pp. 304-305.
[266] *Ibid.*
[267] *Ibid.*, p. 305.

During the first two or three years after the Armistice Agreements were signed, Arab-Israeli friction along the Demarcation Lines was of a minor nature, and usually

> originated from innocent motives. Many Arab refugees, seeing no reason why they should not be able to return to their villages, sought to cross into Israeli territory, Israel, however, not wanting the refugees to return, took forceful measures against them as infiltrators. This strong reaction discouraged most refugees from trying to return home. Nevertheless, some of them, anxious to restore contacts with relatives, to reclaim movable properties, and to harvest their crops, were willing to take the risk.[268]

Aware of its military superiority over its Arab neighbors, Israel seized upon this opportunity as a pretext to attack adjacent Arab states, to intimidate them and to compel them to sanction its forceful seizure of Arab territory by signing a peace treaty.[269]

To justify the use of force against neighboring Arab states without appearing to violate the Armistice Agreements, Israel sought to convince the world that its military attacks upon them were measures of self-defense. So, it pictured the non-violent infiltration of the refugees as an armed assault upon peace-loving Israel by armed bands trained, equipped, and sent across the armistice

---

[268] Khouri, p.183.

[269] From a speech by General Dayan to Israeli Army officers, quoted in Burns, pp. 63-64.

lines by the Arab states. The fact of the matter was that the Arab states were not only not responsible for the infiltration but did everything within their means to discourage it. The government of Jordan, for example, sought to assure Israel that "recent infiltrations into Israel were merely individual cases which are contrary to Jordan's policy and commitments under the GAA [General Armistice Agreement]. Orders have been issued to Jordan forces to open fire on any infiltrator."[270] Measures undertaken by Jordan to curb infiltration also included the increase by 30% of its border police and border patrols, and the authorization of detention of persons even suspected of infiltration.

> In 1954 alone, nearly one thousand infiltrators were sentenced to jail terms, and suspended sentences were given to many others accused of lesser frontier violations... [Jordanian] army trackers cooperated with UN observers and even with Israeli authorities in an attempt to identify and apprehend alleged infiltrators from Jordan.[271]

Nor was Jordan alone in its desire to curb infiltration. "Lebanon moved 9,000 Arab refugees from the border area to prevent infiltrations."[272] And "Egypt also passed laws providing stricter penalties for illegal crossings and generally urged her police and military officials to enforce these laws."[273]

---

[270] Burns, p. 159.
[271] Khouri, p. 186.
[272] Ibid.
[273] Ibid.

Measures undertaken by the Arab states to discourage infiltration were verified by United Nations observers in Palestine.[274] But in spite of all evidence to the contrary, Israel found it useful to hold the Arab states responsible for them and embarked upon a policy of reprisal against them. As a consequence, Israel's victims included not only displaced persons who sought to "infiltrate" back into their own villages, but also the residents of Arab villages near the Armistice lines, who bore the brunt of Israel's reprisal raids even though they never were involved in infiltration incidents.

Instead of lessening the degree of infiltration, Israel's policy of reprisal increased the hostilities and eventually led to armed incursions into Israeli held territory. The fact that "Many Arabs were killed inside Israel while trying to retrieve items from their former homes or harvests from the lands they once had possessed and to which they believed they still held legal title,"[275] caused the refugees to become less and less peaceful. The refugees' previous motivation to "steal" their own property gradually gave way to a desire to inflict injury on those who robbed them of that property.[276]

Israel's irrational response to the problem of refugee infiltration not only resulted in making the infiltrators less peaceful in their intentions, but also created a new breed of infiltrators, the commandos or *fedayeen*, who were infinitely more threatening to Israel's security than the

---

[274] Hutchison, pp. 104-106.
[275] *Ibid.*, p.16.
[276] *Ibid.*, pp. 102-104.

peaceful refugees. In 1955, after five years of no Arab governmental response to Israeli "retaliatory" attacks on Arab border inhabitants, Arab public opinion began to pressure Arab governments into reciprocation. What particularly incensed Arab opinion was the senseless cruelty manifested by the Israeli forces in their attacks on Arab border villages.

For example, on the night of October 14/15, 1953, a sizeable Israeli force attacked the border village of Qibiya in Jordan. The attackers blew up a considerable part of the village and killed 53 men, women, and children. United Nations observers, as the Chief of Staff of UNTSO reported to the Security Council on October 27, revealed during their investigation of the attack that "the inhabitants had been forced to remain inside until their homes were blown up over them."[277]

Repeated condemnations by the Armistice Commissions in Palestine as well as by the United Nations itself failed to deter Israel. Especially after the more militant Ben Gurion who, in the words of the Chief of Staff of UNTSO, "is not exactly a dove of peace,"[278] became Defense Minister in 1954, violations of the Armistice Agreements increased at an alarming rate. By August 1955, complaints of violations on the Israeli-Jordan front alone waiting for consideration by the Jordan-Israel Mixed Armistice Commission totaled 2,150.[279]

---

[277] Hutchison, p. 157.
[278] Burns, p.67.
[279] Ibid., p. 41.

Ben Gurion, who took the arrogant position that the Arabs "best understood sharp words and tough action,"[280] seemed to have little concern for the legality or illegality of his policy or for world public opinion.[281] He was encouraged not only by the ineffectiveness of the United Nations, but also by the fact that he could count on "World Zionism [which] has, thus far, been able to portray Israel in a sympathetic role."[282] The distortion which pictured Israel as the hapless victim of relentless Arab harassment "has allowed Israel to run roughshod over the feelings of her Arab neighbors and to ignore all resolutions adopted by the United Nations that are not to her liking."[283]

Israel's policy of intimidation led, in February 1955, to a major attack on the refugee-packed Gaza Strip, which resulted in the killing of thirty-eight and wounding thirty-one people.[284] The attack was followed by another assault on an Egyptian military post at Khan Yunis, also in the Gaza Strip, in which more than twenty soldiers died.[285]

---

[280] Fred J. Khouri, "The Policy of Retaliation in Arab-Israeli Relations, *The Middle East Journal*, Vol. 20, No, 4, Autumn, 1966, p. 437.

[281] *Ibid*.

[282] Hutchison, p.93.

[283] *Ibid*.

[284] Khouri, "Policy of Retaliation...," p. 440. Also Hutchison, p. 117.

[285] Hutchison, p. 119. Editor's Note: "Israel has fought 15 wars against the Gaza Strip. The number of Gazans killed in the most recent 2023 war — 27,000 — is higher than the death toll of all other wars of the Arab-Israeli conflict." Wikipedia quoted from Liam Stack (21 Dec 2023) *New York Times* and The Associated Press (5 Feb 2024) "Live Updates | Israel strikes raise Gaze death toll as Blinken heads to Mideast", *The Hill*. As of 28 April 2024, the death toll is above 35,000 with no end in sight.

These attacks on the Gaza Strip caused the introduction of two new factors in the situation. First, they compelled Egypt to upgrade its defense capabilities, an effort which, due to the reluctance of the Western powers to sell Egypt the modern arms it needed, led to the much-publicized Czech arms deal in the fall of 1955.[286] Second, the Israeli attacks caused Egyptian public opinion to intensify the demands that the government take countermeasures against Israel. Finally, the Egyptian government yielded to pressure and authorized "small raiding parties in Israel in token reprisal."[287] This was the beginning of the Arab commando (*fedayeen*) movement. Contrary to Israel's well-known claims that its attacks on Arab territory were in retaliation against *fedayeen* attacks on Israel, the fact was that the *fedayeen* were the Arabs' long-delayed response to Israel's policy of intimidation.[288]

In a typical fashion, Israel began to use these two developments (the Czech arms deal and the *fedayeen*) which it had itself provoked, to parade itself before public opinion as the victim of Arab wicked designs, enabling it to pass off as measures of legitimate self-defense two full-scale wars against its Arab neighbors in 1956 and again in 1967.

Israel's conduct toward the Armistice Agreements with the Arab states shows that, on innumerable occasions, it deliberately provoked border incidents to

---

[286] Alfred M. Lilienthal, *There Goes the Middle East.* (New York: The Bookmailer, Inc., 1961), pp.115-127.

[287] *Ibid.* Also Burns, p. 58.

[288] Burns, p. 58, 140.

give itself the pretext it wanted for committing aggression against them without seeming to be guilty of aggression but simply "retaliating" against Arab aggression. Israel has been so successful at this masquerade that its attacks on Arab territory, whether large or small, are always reported by the mass media as "retaliation" or "reprisal."

A few examples of Israel's deliberate provocation of incidents will suffice to illustrate the point. One of Israel's methods of provoking the Arabs into giving it a pretext for "retaliating" is to send an armed patrol deep into Arab territory, and then "retaliate" if the intruders are discovered and killed or captured.[289]

Sometimes, the Israelis sought to justify their irresponsible disregard of the territorial sovereignty of their Arab neighbors with ludicrous explanations. On April 12, 1955, for example, three Israelis were captured about ten kilometers inside Lebanese territory. When they were caught, "they explained that they were just going for a hike," although they admitted knowing that they were in Arab territory. Unfortunately for their story, wrote General Burns, the Chief of Staff of UNTSO, "they had equipped themselves with sub-machine guns, grenades, maps, bully beef, and other military impedimenta which would be considered unusual for a picnic in most countries."[290]

---

[289] See Hutchison, pp. 60-62 for such an act against Jordan and pp, 108-110 for a similar act against Syria. In the incident involving Syria Israel "retaliated" with a major assault resulting in the death of 50 Syrians.

[290] Burns, p. 121.

In contrast, the Arab states not only refrained from sending their soldiers across the armistice lines, but also tried to prevent the possibility that private citizens might give Israel the pretext that it sought. They not only undertook measures to curb infiltration by the refugees, as it was shown earlier, but they also tried to discourage individuals who had been victimized by Israeli "reprisal" raids from taking matters into their own hands and attempting to avenge themselves.

Relating such a case which he witnessed during his service as a U. N. military observer, Commander Hutchison wrote that after the Israeli attack on the Jordanian village of Beit Jalla, he heard a Jordanian lieutenant warn a man who had lost five members of his family during the raid, against attempting revenge.

> I watched carefully as the old man spoke bitterly to the lieutenant. It was not difficult to interpret what he said: "Watch me closely, I'll kill every Israeli I can find!" I don't know that he ever attempted to carry out his threat but I do know that he was soon moved from the border area.[291]

In the fall of 1954, a Bedouin soldier in the Arab Legion "retaliated personally" against Israel for the murder of his cousin—he was arrested and court martialed.[292]

Another method Israel used to provoke incidents along the armistice lines was to send its armed patrols, or

---

[291] Hutchison, p. 104.

[292] Burns, pp. 40-41. The soldier, however, escaped while awaiting sentence, and continued his one-man war on Israel until he was killed.

168

to hold military maneuvers right on the demarcation line. As Lieutenant-General Burns put it:

> The Israelis from time to time carried out military exercises with forces a company or more in strength, advancing towards the demarcation line. On more than one occasion the Arab Legion thought an attack was being mounted upon them, and opened fire, which was, of course, returned, with casualties on both sides.[293]

The same U. N. observer stated his belief that Israel had deliberately provoked the Syrians on December 10, 1955, in Lake Tiberias, and then "retaliated" with a major attack the next day, killing 56 people.[294] United Nations personnel in Palestine repeatedly tried to get both Israel and its Arab neighbors to refrain from sending or stationing their forces right on the armistice lines in the belief that such physical closeness tended to generate friction and often shooting incidents. U.N. officials pressed for such measures particularly in the sensitive Gaza Strip. While Israel refused to do so, Egypt not only accepted, but in some instances unilaterally withdrew its troops back from the armistice lines.[295]

These are some of the ways in which Israel provoked its Arab neighbors into giving it the excuse for carrying out its "reprisals" on which its policy of intimidation was based. But the Arabs could not escape Israel's "retaliation"

---

[293] *Ibid.*, p. 67.
[294] *Ibid.*, p. 107-118; Khouri, *The Arab-Israeli Dilemma*, pp. 195-196.
[295] Khouri, *The Arab-Israeli Dilemma*, p. 185.

even when they failed to get provoked. Israel on many occasions seemed to hold the view that there are no criminals in Israel, and consequently tended to blame the Arabs for crimes committed within the territory under its control. On the basis of his personal experience with the Jordan-Israel Mixed Armistice Commission, Commander Hutchison observed that "even incidents that could not be attributed to Jordan were usually followed by an Israeli raid."[296]

For example, early in 1952, an Israeli woman was raped and killed. Working on the assumption that the criminal was a "marauder" from Jordan, Israel filed a complaint with the Mixed Armistice Commission. The crime was investigated by Major Loreaux, a Belgian member of the Commission, and he found no evidence to justify Israeli suspicions, and suggested that "the Israeli police would have a better chance of finding the killer than the Arabs would."[297] Israel's response, however, was to launch a major "reprisal" attack on the Jordanian village of Beit Jalla.

Another example of Israeli "retaliation" even in the absence of evidence linking the Arab state accused with the incident involved is the Scorpion Pass Incident in 1954. In this incident an Israeli bus was attacked, and several people were killed. United Nations observers investigated the incident with the full cooperation of the Jordanian authorities. Although the investigation concluded that "the evidence did not tie Jordan to the incident," Israel

---

[296] Hutchison, p. 104.
[297] *Ibid.*, p.16.

was so determined to find Jordan guilty that "the tracking dogs were not allowed to circle the area to check other lead offs."[298] In spite of the fact that the investigation failed to implicate Jordan in the crime, Israel nevertheless carried out a major assault on the town of Nahalin.[299]

After the Scorpion Pass Incident, Israel even ceased to file complaints with the Mixed Armistice Commission. It informed the Chief of Staff of UNTSO that "Israel in future would not agree to U. N. observers taking part in the investigation of incidents which occurred inside Israeli-controlled territory."[300] It constituted itself prosecutor, judge, jury, and executioner, and began to respond with "reprisal" raids automatically for crimes committed in its territory, and within three months its aggression netted fifteen condemnations for violations of the Jordan-Israeli Armistice Agreement.[301]

Referring to this attitude of Israel, Secretary-General Hammarskjold told the Security Council that it constituted "a dangerous negation of vital elements of the Armistice Agreement."[302] As the Chief of Staff of UNTSO bluntly put it, Israel gave itself the opportunity to invent incidents whenever it chose to make war against its Arab neighbors.[303]

One more point concerning Israel's behavior towards the Armistice Agreements must be mentioned.

---

[298] *Ibid.*, pp. 53-54.
[299] Khouri, The Arab-Israeli Dilemma, p. 188.
[300] Burns, p. 172.
[301] Hutchison, p. 55.
[302] Burns, p. 172.
[303] *Ibid.*

And that is Israel's consistent obstruction of the efforts of United Nations observers in Palestine to oversee the operations of the Armistice Agreements as they were authorized by the United Nations.

One of the most telling illustrations of Israel's attitude toward the Armistice Agreements and the U. N. representatives in Palestine is taken from Major General Carl von Horn's account of his first meeting with Israeli officials immediately after his appointment as Chief of Staff of UNTSO. Upon his arrival in Palestine, von Horn said, he proceeded to make the usual courtesy calls on the governments of Egypt, Syria, Lebanon, Jordan, and Israel, the parties to the Armistice Agreements. In Israel, he said, he was received by Walter Eytan, the Director General of the Israeli Foreign Ministry. Eytan shocked the newly-arrived Chief of Staff of UNTSO by advising him to "refrain from sticking to the rules of the Armistice Agreements."[304] Von Horn then was handed over to Yosef Tekoah, Israel's Director of Armistice Affairs, who echoed his boss's advice "that I should no longer stick to the rules."[305] What did the Israelis think the function of UNTSO was if it was not the enforcement of the rules of the Armistice Agreements?

It did not take von Horn long on the job to realize the import of Dag Hammarekjold's advice to him when he first accepted the post of Chief of Staff of UNTSO. "Remember that whatever you do," the U. N. Secretary-General had told him, "you will never have the

---

[304] Von Horn, p. 84.
[305] *Ibid.*

wholehearted confidence and cooperation of the Israelis."[306]

Israel has made serious, and often successful, efforts to undermine the integrity and impartiality of U. N. observers in Palestine. Its methods for doing so went all the way up (or down) to and including the use of Israeli women to get U. N. personnel in compromising situations and then blackmailing them.[307]

Another way in which Israel sought to obstruct the functioning of the U. N. Armistice supervisory agencies in Palestine was by playing what amounted to a game of hide and seek with U.N. officials. Israeli officials had a habit of disappearing when U. N. officials sought to confer with them for the purpose of averting an impending border crisis.[308] For example, when Israel was intent on violating the Armistice Agreement with Jordan by holding a military parade which involved the introduction of armed forces into demilitarized zones in Jerusalem, the Chief of Staff of UNTSO sought to avert a possible armed clash between Israel and Jordan by trying to dissuade the Israelis from going through with their illegal and provocative activity. But he could not arrange for a meeting with responsible officials in the Defense Ministry. The U. N. official's efforts were met with the Israeli response that the Chief of Staff of the Israeli Army

---

[306] *Ibid.*, p. 20.

[307] For an account of this and other incidents see Chapter Nine "Intrigue and Infiltration," *Ibid.*, pp. 108-126. For further discussion of Israel's attitude toward U. N. Armistice observers see Chapter X, *Israel vs. the U. N.*, Hutchison, pp. 79-89.

[308] Von Horn, p. 87.

could not be located![309] As the same U. N. official later wrote: "No excuse could have sounded more ridiculous."[310]

The case against Israel and its attitude towards the Armistice Agreement must also include Israel's severe restrictions on the movement of U. N. personnel, and its frequent objections to the establishment of observation posts along the demarcation lines.[311]

Mention must also be made of Israel's violation of the Armistice by setting up military posts in the demilitarized zones, usually thinly disguised as Kibbutzim.[312] Israel has also invaded U. N. headquarters and held its personnel at gun point.[313]

One of the significant points to be made about Israel's behavior toward the Armistice is that, in spite of the fact that it has left few rules unbroken, it "could not understand why anybody condemned it for anything."[314] Israel, which has managed to parade as the pitiful, perpetually persecuted Jew writ large, seems to operate under the premise that the past suffering of Jews puts the Jewish state above the law. No other explanation accounts

---

[309] *Ibid.*, p. 90.

[310] *Ibid.*

[311] Khouri, *The Arab-Israeli Dilemma*, pp. 185-186. Numerous references to Israeli restraints on the movement of U. N. observers are also given by von Horn, Burns, and Hutchison.

[312] Burns, p. 68, pp. 95-97, pp. 154-155; Hutchison, p. 111.

[313] See Hutchison's account of the "Barrel Incident," in which Israel was caught red-handed smuggling weapons into the demilitarized zone contrary to the Armistice Agreement. During this incident, Hutchison wrote, Israel "had left few rules unbroken." pp. 20-29

[314] *Ibid.*, p. 52.

for what another U. N. observer called a "nasty" habit of equating objectivity with anti-Semitism.[315]

This Israeli tendency to exaggerate any criticism of its behavior and to react irrationally to it led a former Chief of Staff of UNTSO to describe it as "a national phobia, an inherent capacity for translating every event into terms of persecution. Inevitably, this state of mind bred vindictiveness."[316] And the Arab people have been for the victims of this vindictiveness for decades. Yet throughout this period, the myth of peaceful Israel desperately trying to hold back the relentless tides of Arab aggression continued to survive miraculously.

Of course, people whose knowledge of Israel was derived from first hand observation rather than from reading second hand Zionist accounts, which constitute the bulk of the available literature on Palestine, have known for a long time that the reality is vastly different from the well-publicized fiction. As Hutchison pointed out, many students of the Arab-Israeli conflict have long suspected that Israel had an interest in a tense border.[317] Numerous motives have been attributed by different observers for Israel's desire to keep the armistice lines crackling with tension. It is the "most effective way of assuring that outside interests remain alert to their obligations to Israel."[318] These outside interests include both foreign countries which feel obligated to keep Israel's

---

[315] Von Horn, p. 304.
[316] Ibid., p. 89.
[317] Hutchison, p. 120.
[318] Ibid.

arsenals well supplied with modern weapons,[319] and
Jewish communities all over the world whose Zionist
ideology obligates them to keep the Israeli treasury
solvent, and through their political influence to see that
Israel's cause is supported in the various capitals of the
world.

Tension along the demarcation lines also serves "to
strengthen national unity in Israel at a time when Israel
was trying to forge hundreds of thousands of Jews with
diverse backgrounds, including many from Arab
countries, into one, unified people."[320] It helps Israel keep
its forces in a high state of readiness and, Israel hopes, it
will be a constant reminder to the Arab states of their
military inferiority, which may persuade them to
acquiesce in the injustice done to the Palestinian Arabs.
But above all, turmoil along the armistice lines has helped
Israel, under the guise of retaliation and the quest for
peace and "secure borders," to mount two major
expansionist drives which ultimately netted for Israel vast
new territory.[321]

This, briefly, has been Israel's record, which more
accurately than its own widely circulated press releases,
depicts its attitude toward the question of how peace can

---

[319] As the *New York Times* correspondent in Israel put it on April
22, 1956, Israel is afraid that quiet along the armistice lines "will
strengthen the Eisenhower administration's ability to resist internal
pressures for sending arms to Israel. It also fears an illusion of peace
will make arms hard to get from Western Powers" Khouri, *The Arab-Israeli Dilemma*, p. 189.

[320] Khouri, *The Arab-Israeli Dilemma*, p. 189.

[321] Israeli expansionism will be discussed in the following
chapter.

be restored to the Middle East. Israel's incessant proclamations that it desired peace with its neighbors were belied by its aggressive behavior toward them. But the proclamations were well publicized; the deeds were known only to a few people outside the Middle East. The few who had the opportunity to see for themselves and reach their own conclusions soon discovered "that few, if any, of Israel's past offers of peace were matched by deeds that would invite cooperation."[322]

Israel was not, and is not yet, ready for peace. For it is still a dissatisfied state, and it will remain so until the territorial limits for which it aspires are finally attained.

---

[322] Hutchison, p. 92.

CHAPTER 10 - TERRITORIAL EXPANSION

> Every State consists of a land and a people. Israel is no exception, but it is a State identical neither with its land nor with its people.
> —David Ben Gurion

The true measure of the type and the degree of the confusion with which Israel has managed to surround its true objectives can be seen from the fact that amidst the incessant expressions of fear for the survival of Israel and its people, Israel emerges, many decades after its establishment, not only alive but stronger and, more significantly, much larger. The fact that Israel has, by the use of violence, enormously expanded the territory under its control is beyond debate.[323] But what the Zionists cannot deny they attempt to explain away. It appears that Israel and its friends abroad have in fact succeeded in convincing large segments of world public opinion that, like the British empire in the nineteenth century, the new Zionist empire in the Arab World was built in a fit of absent mindedness. The growth of Israel from the half of Palestine in 1948 to all of Palestine plus the Sinai

---

[323] See following set of 3 [s depicting the progressive territorial expansion of Israel in the first 20 years of its existence. Image licensed by iStock photo credit to Dimitrios Karamitros.

Peninsula and the southwestern part of Syria was never intended, it is asserted. It just happened that way.

Israel hinges its assertion that its territorial expansion was not intended on the claim that all its wars against the Arabs have been wars of self-defense. No one reading this book is likely to be unfamiliar with Israel's widely publicized explanation of its expansion. But it may be useful to restate it briefly. Israel's argument is as follows:

When the Arabs failed to obstruct the passage of the United Nations General Assembly resolution of November 29, 1947, recommending the partition of Palestine and the establishment of a Jewish state in a part thereof, they sought to prevent its implementation by force of arms. As soon as Britain completed its evacuation of Palestine in mid-May 1948, the Arab states invaded the country in an effort to prevent the Jews from proclaiming a state in the part of Palestine allocated to them by the United Nations. The Jews defeated the Arab invaders and, by the time an armistice was arranged to end the fighting in 1949, the Jews not only managed to preserve their state but also found their forces in control of a larger portion of Palestine than the partition resolution gave to them.

Since the Jews paid for the extra land with their blood, and the Arabs continued to be unreconciled to the existence of a Jewish state in Palestine, Israel could not very well return the conquered territory to the Arabs. Moreover, the Arabs left their lands and hundreds of thousands of Jewish immigrants came and settled in their place, making it even more unreasonable to expect Israel to give up the land.

Continued Arab threats and provocation of Israel compelled it in 1956 and again in 1967 to fight "preventive" wars which resulted not only in the defeat of the Arab would-be aggressors, but also in the loss of more territory to Israel. Israel is not nor was it ever interested in the acquisition of Arab territory. All it wanted was to be left alone by its neighbors. But in view of continued Arab hostility toward it, Israel cannot, without jeopardizing its survival, return to the Arabs all of the territories it took from them in the 1967 war. Israel has to give itself "secure borders" by holding on to strategic territories like the Golan Heights of Syria and others which prior to the 1967 war enabled Arab forces to pose a mortal danger to Israel and its citizens.

This is the essence of Israel's argument which helped it expand enormously without appearing to be deliberately expansionist. The propagation of this explanation of Israel's territorial aggrandizement has been the main task of the Israeli Foreign Ministry and its auxiliaries at home and abroad since the inception of the state of Israel. This helps explain the curious fact that, contrary to normal practice, Israel's Foreign Ministry is, and has always been, the handmaiden of its Defense Ministry. As Major General Burns, former Chief of Staff of UNTSO, commented on the Israeli announcement justifying Israel's attack on Egypt in the fall of 1956:

> I was reminded again of the words I had heard attributed to Mr. Ben-Gurion a year and a half before: that the function of the Ministry of Foreign Affairs was to justify, in the eyes of the

world, the actions of the Israeli Defense Forces.[324]

In plain words, Israel periodically wages wars of conquest, seizes more territory, annexes it, and explains the whole thing as an act of self-defense. This *modus operandi* has been so successful that an observer of Israeli expansionism concluded that "Seldom in modern times has self-defense proved to be such a profitable undertaking."[325]

To fulfill its task of justifying to the world the actions of Israel's armed forces, the Israeli Foreign Ministry has to distort and to invent outright fictions. The distortion is necessary for two related reasons. First, there is a large gap between the facts of Israel's behavior and the fiction which it seeks to propagate. Second, Israel's success in its expansionist drive depends to a great extent on the support of outsiders, both Jews and non-Jews, most of whom would withhold their support from Israel if the truth about its true objectives were known to them.

It is imperative for anyone who seeks to penetrate the deep layers of fog generated by Israel's highly efficient propagandists and to look beyond it at the true state of affairs in Palestine to realize that Israeli deception on the question of territorial gains goes beyond the charges-and-counter-charges routine in which all states occasionally

---

[324] Burns, p. 181.

[325] Howard Koch, Jr., *Six Hundred Days: A Reappraisal of the Arab-Israeli Confrontation Since June,1967* (A Memorial issued by the Permanent Observer of the League of Arab States to the United Nations, March 1969), p.45.

indulge. It is a policy deliberately pursued and skillfully executed.

As Howard Koch put it in connection with his discussion of Israel's tortured search for a justification for its initiative in the 1967 war: "It is not a pleasant task to charge a government or its representatives with deliberate deception, but circumstances leave us with no alternative."[326] Most people, of course, have no way of ascertaining the truth of assertions they read or hear about events in other lands. But when one sees disinterested witnesses, like the United Nations observers on the scene, with practical unanimity begin with their sympathy on Israel's side and then, after years of first-hand observation, are repelled by Israel's deception, one begins to at least doubt. And such observers of Israel have been unequivocal in their conclusions.

As Carl von Horn expressed his own and other U. N. observers' feelings after witnessing Israel's distortion of events:

> We [the personnel of UNTSO in Palestine] were amazed at the ingenuity of the falsehoods that distorted the true picture. The highly skilled Israeli information service and the entire press combined to manufacture a

---

[326] *Ibid.*, p. 19. See his account of how, in the initial stage of the war, Israeli official representatives in the United Nations actually lied to the international organization and the world, including their own people. by announcing that Israel went to war on the morning of June 5 to repel a land and air attack initiated by Egypt against Israel. Later, in the face of overwhelming evidence, Israel had to retract and issue a different justification for its offensive strike against the Arab states. pp. 11-19.

warped, distorted version that was disseminated with professional expertise through every available channel to their own people and their sympathizers and supporters in America and the rest of the world. Never in all my life had I believed the truth could be so cynically, expertly bent.327

Israel's skillful portrayal of expansionism as the unintended consequence of self-defense gained for it the support and sympathy of millions of people who had not the slightest interest, motive, or intention of being partners of Zionism in its assault on the Arab people. It even caused many governments, particularly the government of the United States, to lend their support to policies which are both unjust and contrary to their own national interests. United States Colonel William T. McAninch, who had served as the Military Assistant to the Chief of Staff of UNTSO, wrote in reference to Israel's campaign of deception and its consequences to America: "Zionism has seemingly blinded large numbers...of American Jewry and exploited the ignorance and apathy of the majority of Americans. Today, United States relations with the Middle East are in grave jeopardy as a result."328

The success of Israel's campaign of deceit cannot be wholly attributed to the skill of its propagandists, although their skill must be conceded. Many other factors help to give Israel an overwhelming advantage in the field

---

327 Von Horn, p. 95.
328 Hutchison, pp. ix-x.

of propaganda over the Arabs. The following three factors are perhaps the most important:

First, the fact that the Israelis are far outnumbered by the Arabs makes it difficult for people to visualize Israel in the role of the aggressor. In view of the large disparity between the population of Israel and the aggregate populations of the several Arab states, Israel appears to be taking grave risks by provoking its neighbors, which leads people to conclude that the provocation must come from the Arab side. In contrast, it is much easier and much more reasonable in view of' population statistics, to picture Arab "hordes" descending upon little Israel with thoughts of revenge. In spite of the fact that the importance of technology in modern warfare is universally recognized, and the fact that the technological superiority of the Europeans who inhabit Israel is well known, the possibility of an impending conflict between Israel and its Arab neighbors still conjures up the usual vision of charging Arab hordes.

But in warfare total numbers do not count, only mobilized and utilized resources do. And the image of little Israel menaced by Arab hordes survives primarily because of the general ignorance of the fact that in *all its wars with its neighbors Israel has in fact outnumbered all of. the Arab states in terms of the number of combatants deployed for battle.* All available evidence indicates that, in the first Arab-Israeli war in 1947-1949, Israeli forces outnumbered Arab forces by at least two to one, and some estimates put the Arabs at a greater numerical disadvantage.[329] The second large-scale Arab-Israeli armed clash, commenced with Israel's invasion of the Egyptian Sinai Peninsula and the Gaza Strip, took the form of an Anglo-French-Israeli alliance against Egypt. And in the third Arab-Israeli war, in 1967, Israel again was able to mobilize and deploy a larger force than the participating Arab states combined.[330]

The fiction of little Israel surrounded by a sea of hostile Arabs threatening its existence, therefore, helps give credence to Israel's peaceful pretensions, but it hardly deters Israel which is fully aware of the facts.[331] The numerical superiority of the Israeli forces, coupled with the fact that Israel has always enjoyed the advantage of an initial strike, lead to the conclusion that the widespread mistaken belief that Israel's military inferiority precludes an aggressive posture on the part of Israel is untenable and is not supported by the evidence available.[332]

---

[329] Nutting, *The Arabs*, p. 330: Khouri, *The Arab-Israeli Dilemma,* pp. 70-72. Other authors give estimates as high as six to one. For details see Chapter 8.

[330] Khouri, *The Arab-Israeli Dilemma,* footnote 44, p. 401.

[331] A few months after the war of June 1967, Israel's General Rabin admitted in an interview with the French newspaper *Le Monde* on February 28, 1968, that Egypt had neither the intention nor the forces to attack Israel. He said, "I do not believe that Nasser wanted war. The two divisions he sent into Sinai on May 14 would not have been enough to unleash an offensive against Israel. He knew it and we knew it." Quoted in Kock, p. 31.

[332] It has been suggested, in reference to the 1967 war, that "The expectation that the U. S. would probably come to their rescue in case of an unexpected military setback which would threaten their

The second factor which aids Israel's effort to portray its expansionist wars as wars of self-defense is that the traditional stereotype of the Jewish people as a continually harassed people lends itself perfectly to the desired image of a constantly harassed Jewish state. People find it much easier to visualize Israel as the persecuted rather than the persecutor. As it was stated repeatedly in this book, the Zionists were always aware of the benefit to be derived from the persecution of the Jews. From the moment Theodor Herzl wrote *The Jewish State* until this day, the Zionists saw that the suffering of the Jews could be turned into capital.[333] And one of the ways in which this is done is by making it seem rather unnatural to think of Jews as aggressors and persecutors.

Many people supported the idea of a Jewish state on what they honestly believed to be humanitarian grounds. Such people often find themselves troubled by the thought that they helped create an oppressive, aggressive force when confronted with the facts. Some of them resolve this moral dilemma by discontinuing their support of Zionism.[334] Others choose to dismiss the evidence as Arab propaganda or as anti-Semitic diatribes. Mindful of the ever-present possibility that any criticism of Israel might be labeled anti-Semitism, Burns stated in

---

survival probably encouraged the Israeli leaders to take a more daring, all-out offensive gamble." Khouri, *Arab-Israeli Dilemma*, p. 261.

[333] Herzl wrote in *The Jewish State*, "Everything depends on our propelling force. And what is that force? The misery of the Jews." p. 70.

[334] For example, the late columnist Dorothy Thompson, and many U. N. observers, as indicated in the previous chapter.

the preface to his book *Between Arab and Israeli* that "criticism of the policy of the Israeli Government will probably result in a charge of anti-Semitism," to which potential charge he pleaded not guilty.[335] Burns then continued to explain that would have needed no explanations or apologies had his subject dealt with any state other than Israel. From the premise that anti-Semitism is bad, he wrote, "it does not follow that the acts of the Government of Israel and of individual Israelis are not subject to moral judgement; that we have not the right to say whether they are good or bad, helpful or harmful to world peace and justice between nations."[336] Such has been the use that the Zionists have made of "the misery of the Jews" that it has become a widely established rule that Israel's conduct cannot be questioned without incurring grave risks to one's moral reputation.

The third important factor which helps Israel gain acceptance of its version of events is that unlike other countries, which may have supporters and sympathizers in other lands, Israel has in addition to the expected coterie of supporters and large number of *loyalists* in practically every country in the world. These loyalists, the Zionist Jews, often occupy positions in the mass media, in the academic world, in the economy, in the armed forces, in political parties, in labor unions, and in the government, which enable them to be of immense service to Israel. And their Zionist ideology gives them the motive to serve its interests. In free, democratic societies

---

[335] Burns, p. 5.
[336] *Ibid.*, p. 6.

187

especially, as in the United States, Britain, and France, Zionist Jews often behave in a way which indicates that they consider their primary loyalty to be to Israel rather than to the countries of which they are citizens.

A revealing episode illustrating Zionist attitudes on the question of the proper role of the Jew in the country of his citizenship took place during the 1964 elections in the United States. William F. Haddad and Leonard Farbstein were opposing each other as candidates for the Democratic Party nomination for U. S. Congress from the 19th Congressional District of New York. During the campaign, Haddad was "accused" of not being a Jew, but really an Arab, and "Can you trust an Arab," the campaign literature rhetorically asked the prospective Jewish voters of New York, "to fight for the interests of Jews and for Israel?"[337] Apparently it did not occur to Haddad to protest that the proper function of a U. S. Congressman was not "to fight for the interests of the Jews and for Israel." Instead, his defense consisted of an attempt to convince his constituents that he was as reliable as his opponent as a fighter for Israel's interests. He said that the proof of his loyalty is shown by the fact that "he had attempted unsuccessfully as a teenager to volunteer for service in the Haganah, the underground army that fought for the Israeli independence."[338]

The Zionists consciously inculcate a feeling of loyalty to Israel among Jewish people who are citizens of other countries. In the United States, Jewish children have

---

[337] *New York Times,* May 11, 1964, p.26.
[338] *Ibid.,* June 1, 1964, p. 21,

been taught to think of Israel as their country.[339] They have been taught in Sunday schools to take a pledge no other Americans take: "I pledge my loyalty to God, to the Torah and to the Jewish people and to the Jewish state..."[340]

Zionists are fond of saying that Zionism does not implicate them of double loyalties, and that such a charge is a figment of their opponents' imagination. But if a Zionist who lives outside Israel is not guilty of double loyalties, it is only because he reserves all of his loyalty to the State of Israel. No clearer statement of this fact is found than Ben Gurion's own assertion that "when a Jew [meaning a Zionist] in America or South Africa speaks of 'our Government' to his fellow- Jews, he usually means the Government of Israel."[341]

As a consequence, Israel has millions of loyalists throughout the world who often use their positions in government, the press and other points of influence to aid Israel in its campaign of deceit. It is not surprising, therefore, that Israel was able in the short period it has existed to forcibly increase its territory by about 500% and continues to pass itself off as the one country in the Middle East dedicated to peace and coexistence with its neighbors.

---

[339] A survey of 200 American high school students between the ages of 15 and 16, reported by Charles G. Spiegler in the *Chicago Jewish Forum*, Quoted in Lilienthal, *What Price Israel*, p. 231.

[340] From *Sunday School Life*, Washington Heights, New York, Sunday School of the Y. H. M. A. and the Y. H. W. A., quoted in Lilienthal. *Ibid.*, p.232.

[341] David Ben-Gurion. "Jewish Survival," State of Israel, *Government Yearbook* (1953-54), p. 35.

* * *

The whole history of the Zionist movement can be told in terms of Jewish acquisition of Arab land disguised in many forms but seldom in its true character as territorial aggrandizement. Although we are here interested in the territorial expansion of Israel since its establishment in 1948, it is significant to note that even before they succeeded in creating a Jewish state in Palestine, the Zionists tended to make their objectives appear to be less aggressive and acquisitive than they were in fact. This can be seen from the fact that although the World Zionist Movement was created in 1897 to implement Theodor Herzl's idea for the establishment of a Jewish state, the Zionists gave the impression that it was not a state which they sought, but only a refuge, a haven from European persecution. They neither asked for, nor did they receive, an endorsement for a "Jewish state" in Palestine. In fact, the President of the World Zionist Organization wrote immediately after the issuance of the Balfour Declaration that "It has been said, and is being obstinately repeated by anti-Zionists again, that Zionism aims at the creation of an independent 'Jewish state.' But this is wholly fallacious. The 'Jewish state' was never a part of the Zionist programme."[342]

Until Hitler generated a great deal of sympathy for the Jews,

> The Zionists, at least in their more formal demands, had been careful to avoid

[342] Quoted in Lilienthal, *Ibid.*, p 24 from Nahum Sakolow's two volume *History of Zionism,* written in 1918.

specifically requesting a Jewish state—despite the fact that a state was indeed their ultimate goal. Zionist leaders were willing to take one step at a time and achieve their objective piecemeal.[343]

Regardless of what the vague term "national home" may have meant to Zionist leaders in the early stages of their scheme to create an empire in the Arab world, the fact remains that it did sound rather harmless to many people and helped generate support for and neutralize opposition to the Zionist scheme. It helps explain why the authors of the Balfour Declaration felt it was not inconsistent to say, in the same paragraph, that the British government supported the establishment of a national home for the Jews in Palestine and that it opposed the infringement of the rights of the Arabs of Palestine. It explains Prince Faisal's much publicized offer of welcome to Jews wishing to come and live with the Arabs after World War I.[344] It explains why countless millions who had not the slightest desire to displace the Arabs of Palestine became proponents of Zionist ideology.

This early Zionist tendency to conceal and deny its ultimate objectives while pursuing ostensibly less ambitious steps leading to it has been the *modus operandi* of the Zionist movement before and since the establishment of a Jewish state in Palestine. But while deception before the 1940's involved an attempt to conceal

---

[343] Khouri, The Arabi-Israeli Dilemma, p. 6.
[344] See his letter to Justice Frankfurter, dated March 3, 1919, in Chaim Weizmann. *Trial and Error.* (New York: Harper & Brothers, 1949), pp. 245-246.

the fact that it was a territorial state which they sought, it later involved the territorial extent of the ultimate, fully developed Jewish state. Both the words and deeds of Zionist leaders, before and after the establishment of a Jewish state, confirm their commitment to a territorial state larger than that envisioned by the 1947 U. N. partition resolution, larger than the expanded Israel of 1949, and larger than the much-expanded Israel which emerged from the June, 1967 war.

If there is any doubt concerning the territorial expansionist ambitions of Israel, such doubts exist in regard to the exact boundaries which it seeks to reach. But there are no doubts whatsoever that such boundaries have not yet been gained. And it is equally certain that Israel will not in reality seek peace with its neighbors until such boundaries are finally reached. Until then, Israel will continue to wave the synthetic olive branch which has so far served its purposes so well.

* * *

Let us now turn to the question of the size, or territorial extent, of the Jewish state which the Zionist movement envisioned. The first clue to the size of the projected Zionist state comes from Theodor Herzl, the founder of the Zionist Movement, who made several references in his *Diaries* to the size of the projected Zionist state.

Herzl, although he "permitted himself to be both elastic and vague"[345] on the question of the territorial

---

[345] Ben Halpern, *The Idea of the Jewish State* (Cambridge, Mass.: Harvard University Press, 1961) , p. 303.

extent of the future Jewish state, was naturally committed to the proposition that the state must be large enough to absorb all the Jews "in Exile." In Zionist terminology, of course, that means all the Jews in the world. This commitment can be seen from Herzl's answer to a question by Prince Hohenlohe, the German Imperial Chancellor, during a meeting of the two which took place while Herzl was seeking a German endorsement of the concept of a Jewish state. The Chancellor asked Herzl what territory the Zionists wanted, and whether it reached as far north as Beirut or even farther. "I said," wrote Herzl in his *Diaries*, "We will ask for what we need. The more immigrants, the more land."[346]

The official Zionist statement on the subject was embodied in the World Zionist Organization's demands, formally submitted to the victorious Allies who met in Paris in 1919 to determine the fate of Arab lands recently freed from Turkish colonialism. One of the major provisions of the proposals submitted to the Paris Peace Conference concerned the question of boundaries.

Acting on the basic Zionist tenet that all Jews are actually or potentially persecuted people, the Zionists wanted a state capable of solving this "Jewish problem." This state, therefore, must be large enough to accommodate all the Jews of the world, and it must be economically viable. For these reasons, the required territory must include not only all of Palestine, but also southern Lebanon to Sidon, the southwestern part of Syria to the outskirts of Damascus, and the arable land east of

---

[346] Herzl, *Dairies*, p. 257.

the River Jordan to the Hidjaz Railway (i.e. to the desert).[347]

The inclusion of these territories would not only enlarge the territory but would also make it more viable economically since they include all the major sources of water in and around Palestine. They include the Lebanese Litany River, the sources of the Jordan River (on the southern slopes of Mount Hermon in Syria), the headwaters of the Yarmuk River (between Syria and Jordan) and the Jordan River and its tributaries on both sides of the river.

The boundaries of the Jewish State for which the Zionist Organization was asking included not only all of Palestine, but also substantial territories from Lebanon, Syria, and Jordan east of the River Jordan. This statement of the territorial extent of the Jewish state which the Zionists planned to carve out of the Arab world was slightly more modest than a delineation of the boundaries of that state made about a year earlier by two prominent Zionist leaders who later became the two highest office holders in the state of Israel.

In April 1918, an article written by David Ben Gurion, later Prime Minister of Israel, and Yitzhak Ben Zvi, later President of Israel, appeared in *Palestine*, a publication of the Zionist British Palestine Committee, in which the authors discussed the area and boundaries of the projected Jewish state. In this article, the authors included all of Palestine, the southern portion of Lebanon,

---

[347] Halpern, p. 304.

the southwestern part of Syria. and the arable land east of the River Jordan to the rim of the desert.[348]

Although the Zionists have never been in full agreement on the exact area and boundaries of the Jewish state, all of them have always been in agreement that it must include not only Palestine, but also territories from the Arab states around Palestine. When the Zionists speak of a Jewish state in Palestine, people not familiar with Zionism assume that the territory sought is confined within the boundaries of Palestine as the mapmakers know it. What is not generally realized is that the Palestine with which everyone is familiar (the Palestine which is bounded by the Mediterranean, Lebanon, Syria, the River Jordan and the Dead Sea, and the Sinai Peninsula) is not the Palestine that the Zionists have in mind.

The Palestine which is in the Zionist mind is a much larger country. In fact. Zionist writers often speak of Palestine that the maps show as "Western Palestine," the rest of it being east of the River Jordan.[349] This attitude is not confined to the "extremists," like the Herut Party which openly advocates expansionism. In the official Israeli Yearbook of 1952, for example, Prime Minister Ben Gurion wrote that "the state of Israel has been resurrected in the western part of the Land" of Israel.[350] In an article

---

[348] *Palestine,* vol. 3, No. 17, quoted in Abd el Wahab Kayyali, *Zionist Expansionist Ambitions,* Palestine Studies, No. 3, Research Center, Palestine Liberation Organization, Beirut, 1966, pp. 78-79. (in Arabic).

[349] For example, Katz, *Days of Fire,* and Menachem Begin, *The Revolt.*

[350] David Ben-Gurion, "Israel Among the Nations," State of Israel, *Government Yearbook* (1952), p. 13.

written for the 1951-52 issue of the same official publication, Ben Gurion wrote, "we have reached the beginning of independence in a part of our small country."[351] This is the reason why the Zionist prefers to speak of "Eretz Israel" rather than of "Palestine."

The Zionists' commitment to the inclusion of Lebanese, Syrian, and Jordanian territory within the projected Jewish state led them to object to the proclamation of the independence of Trans-Jordan in 1922 as an Arab state on the ground that it constituted a division of "Eretz Israel."[352] They similarly objected to the exclusion of the southern parts of Syria and Lebanon for the same reasons.[353]

As far as the southern boundary of the projected Jewish state was concerned, the Zionists tended to be rather inconsistent on whether or not they wished to include the Sinai Peninsula. In their presentations to the Paris Peace Conference, the Zionists seemed to be satisfied with a line extending from Aqaba to El Arish, thus disavowing the intention to incorporate the Peninsula into the future Zionist state.[354] Occasionally, however, Zionist leaders indicated that they had reservations about conceding Egypt's ownership of the area. Ben Gurion had repeatedly expressed the view that Egyptian territory began beyond the Suez Canal.[355]

---

[351] David Ben-Gurion, "The Call of Spirit in Israel," State of Israel, *Government Yearbook* (1951-52), p. x.

[352] Katz, *Days of Fire*, p. 72.

[353] Kayyali, p. 85, and Halpern, p. 278.

[354] Halpern, p. 304.

[355] Ben Gurion, *Israel: Years of Challenge*, p. 120, 125, 126.

Of course, there have been moments when Zionist leaders betrayed a desire to see their projected state extend even beyond these boundaries which they officially endorsed. In line with their habit of justifying their political ambitions on religious grounds, they tended at times to dream of an empire extending from the Nile to the Euphrates as a fulfillment of their understanding of the Old Testament's prescription that "your territory shall be from the wilderness to Lebanon and from the River, the river Euphrates, to the western sea."[356] In one of his more optimistic moods. Theodor Herzl wrote in his Diaries: "The northern frontier is to be the mountains facing Cappadocia; the southern, the Suez Canal. Our slogan shall be: The Palestine of David and Solomon!"[357]

These territorial claims made by the Zionist Movement were never subsequently disclaimed or modified. In 1948, a beginning was made in the realization of Zionist plans by the establishment of a Jewish state in a relatively small area covering slightly over half of Palestine. Twenty years later, the beachhead had grown to such an extent that the Jewish state is beginning to approximate the original design. But the present "boundaries" of Israel still fall short of the boundaries envisioned for it. The major pieces of territory which are still to be conquered consist of southern Lebanon, on to the Litany River, and the strip of arable land east of the River Jordan.

---

[356] Deuteronomy, 11:24.
[357] Herzl, *Diaries,* p. 124.

It may be argued, of course, that the territorial definition of the Jewish state sought by the Zionist Movement in the time of Herzl is not necessarily the same as that pursued by the Zionist Movement today or by its child, the state of Israel. It must be conceded that it is impossible to prove or to disprove, to everyone's satisfaction, that further expansion will in fact be attempted.[358] But in a case of this sort, the expectation of such a proof is logically untenable. A judgment must necessarily be based on the availability of evidence indicating a continued commitment to the territorial aspects of "Eretz Israel" as the Zionist Movement had originally envisioned it. Such evidence is available, and it is derived from the words and deeds of Zionist-Israeli leaders and spokesmen, in and out of office.

There is no evidence to suggest that the Zionist acceptance of the U. N. partition resolution signified an abandonment of the territorial demands to which the Zionist movement committed itself in the first fifty years of its existence. The more extremists among them made no secret of their rejection of the resolution which, by not endorsing Zionist claims to all of Palestine, was rendered

---

[358] I began working on this book several years ago. I discussed it with several colleagues presumed to be knowledgeable in Arab-Israeli relations. They expressed skepticism about my views on Israeli expansionism. Shortly after that, the 1967 war and the enormous extension of territory came. [Editor's note: This footnote was written in 1969, just before the author returned to Jordan, and later to Occupied Palestine as professor, dean, and later as Vice-President for Academic Affairs of Birzeit University.]

illegal in their eyes.[359] The Zionists argued that they had an inherent right to Palestine derived from the historical fact that they once had a state there, and that, therefore, the United Nations was recognizing rather than granting that right in its partition resolution.[360] For this reason they saw no inconsistency in their acceptance of those parts of the resolution which confirmed the inherent right they thought they had and their rejection of the parts of the same resolution which they believed to be in conflict with their claims. Thus they welcomed the recommendation that a Jewish state be established in Palestine, but rejected the validity of the confinement of that state to a part of the country.

But while the "extremists" among the Zionists were frank in their feelings on this matter, the official representatives of the Zionist movement were no less committed to the proposition that the partition of Palestine must not be accepted as a final settlement. As it was pointed out in Chapter 8, the military objectives of the Haganah, the military arm of the Jewish Agency in Palestine, were geared to the extension rather than the mere defense of the territory allocated to the Jewish state by the U. N. partition resolution.

Years after the 1947-1949 Arab-Israeli war ended, Israeli leaders were still blaming each other for the failure

---

[359] "The partition of the Homeland is illegal, It will never be recognized." Begin, p. 335.

[360] An Israeli writer formerly affiliated with the Irgun put it this way, "To the Irgun a United Nations decision for a Jewish state was not a charter of independence but a recognition of our rights." Katz, *Days .of Fire*, p. 180.

to occupy all of Palestine. The significant thing about this debate is that no Israeli leader had taken the position that he felt it was wrong to expand the territory of the state. The politicians blamed the inefficiency of the soldiers and the soldier's blamed the blundering of the politicians, but neither side would admit that it did not wish to occupy all of Palestine or even accuse the other side of deliberately renouncing this common goal.

In an interview with the Israeli newspaper *Haboker* on March 6, 1964, Ben Gurion declared that "if he had other generals — specifically General Moshe Dayan — in 1948 our frontiers might well have been different," implying that "he had wanted to occupy all western Palestine [in non-Zionist terminology, all of Palestine] but had been frustrated in his determination by the inefficiency of the soldiers."[361] To this explanation of why the Zionists failed to occupy all of Palestine, the soldiers responded that they "longed to liberate the entire country" but were prevented from doing so by "mistaken political decisions."[362]

Whether it was the inefficiency of the soldiers or the fumbling of the politicians which kept them from expanding the territory of their state in 1948, the Zionists are emphatic in their protestations that it was not their lack of desire which was to blame. In their intimate conversations with each other, the Zionists did not conceal the fact that they were fighting to extend the size of their state. Even before the Zionists proclaimed a state

---

[361] Katz, p. 261.
[362] *Ibid.*

in Palestine in mid-May 1948, they made their expansionist intentions clear. In April 1948, for example, the Irgun sent an agent to the United States to secure financial support for the Zionist war effort. The agent met with Rabbi Abba Hillel Silver, the leader of American Zionists, and explained to him that the "strategic purpose" of the war was "canceling the frontiers of partition,"[363] with which objective the American Zionist leader had no quarrel.

There is no doubt that the widely publicized account that it was a war of self-defense which the Zionists were fighting in 1948 was manufactured strictly for export. It was necessary for gaining the diplomatic and financial support which the Zionists needed to carry out their territorial conquest of Palestine.

This initial spurt of expansionism increased Israel's territory by about 30%. But 80% of Palestine's territory fell short of satisfying the Zionist movement's territorial ambitions. Even after the expulsion of the majority of Palestine's Arabs from the territory which the Zionist forces occupied, the territory was still too small to enable the Zionists to implement their solution to the "Jewish problem," which required that all the Jews of the world be saved from Gentile claws by "ingathering" them into the Jewish state.

After this first expansionist phase ended with the establishment of Armistice Agreements in 1949, Israel's territorial expansion continued with the assertion of

---

[363] *Ibid.*, p. 210.

sovereignty over the various demilitarized zones.[364] But the incorporation of these zones presented a small territorial gain and did not bring Israel's borders to where the Zionist movement sought to place them—far beyond the traditional borders of Palestine. Nor did they give Israel the *lebensraum* it was preparing for the millions of Jews Israel's agents throughout the world sought to transplant to Palestine.[365]

The second opportunity for a major territorial expansionist effort presented itself in the mid 1950's. Continuous Israeli provocation, especially in the Gaza Strip, finally compelled the Arabs to respond by organizing commando units and by seeking and obtaining modern arms for their regular forces.[366] Using these defense responses as "proof" of hostile intent, Israel launched a propaganda campaign to convince the world that it was in mortal danger, and thus paved the way for an all-out war against Egypt in the fall of 1956, which again it justified as a preventive war of self-defense. It occupied the Gaza Strip and most of the Sinai Peninsula.

Israel's claims that it fought to destroy Egyptian arms in the Sinai Peninsula and the commando bases in the Gaza Strip became less convincing when it resisted pressures to withdraw after successfully achieving the announced objectives of the war. Also, its claims were further weakened by the fact that it refused to permit the

---

[364] See Chapter 9.

[365] For an account of the methods used to induce Jews to go to Palestine, See Chapter XI, "Operation 'Ingathering'" in Lilienthal, *What Price Israel?*, pp. 191-212.

[366] See Chapter 9.

U. N. truce supervisors to verify its claims that it was being harassed by Arab commando intrusions in its territory. As the then Chief of Staff of UNTSO put it: "as there was no impartial investigation of the facts, it was open to the Israeli authorities, if they wanted a *casus belli*, to exaggerate or falsify any incident, or even to invent incidents."[367]

Israel's claims that it fought in self-defense were further undermined by the fact that it marched against Egypt as a partner in an alliance with France and Britain, who were making a last-ditch effort to save the remnants of their crumbling colonial systems. Israel's inability to convince the world that its occupation of Arab territory was a measure of self-defense cost it diplomatic support which it needed to hold on to the fruits of its aggression. Consequently, it withdrew from the occupied territories.

Ten years after this abortive attempt to enlarge its territory, Israel engineered its most successful expansionist effort to date. Again, under the cover of self-defense, Israel launched all-out war against surrounding Arab territory and occupied the remaining part of Palestine, the Sinai Peninsula, and the Syrian Golan Heights, and vouched that the map would never again look as it did before the war.

To assure itself that, unlike in 1956, it would have the diplomatic support it needed to hold on to the territory it occupied, Israel in 1967 provoked the Arabs into a posture of apparent belligerency which caused external public

---

[367] Burns, p. 181.

opinion to buy its explanation that it was compelled to fight a war of self-defense.

After a series of serious violations of the Armistice agreements for which Israel was condemned by the Security Council, including an attack on a village of Es-Samo in Jordan, highly placed Israeli officials began to make public threats against the Arab states which compelled them to take defensive precautions, which Israel promptly presented to the world as proof of hostile Arab intent. By quoting *parts* of statements made by Arab officials, the Israelis make it appear that the Arabs were indeed preparing to attack Israel. In presenting Israel's attack on the Arab states as a clear act of self-defense, for example, the Israeli Foreign Minister told the Security Council that he had heard "with my very own ears" a radio speech by President Nasser in which he said: "We intend to open a general assault against Israel. This will be total war." What President Nasser had in fact said was that: *"If Israel embarks on an aggression against Syria or Egypt,* the battle against Israel will be a general one and not confined to one spot on the Syrian or Egyptian borders..."[368]

What the Arabs were threatening in other words, was *resistance* to Israeli aggression should it come, and not an aggressive war against Israel. But the Arab case did not reach the foreign publics, and when it did, it reached them through the distorting intermediary of Israel's agents and loyalists. Thus, the Arabs were cast in the role of the

---

[368] Koch, p. 14.

villain, and when Israel launched its war, it found little difficulty in portraying it as a war of self-defense.

Israel's deception went even further than the mere distortion of statements made by Arab spokesman. When the 1967 war broke out, Israel initially attempted to deny that it initiated it. The Israeli representative to the United Nations informed the Security Council on June 5, that "fighting had erupted on Israel's frontiers" and continued to say:

> I have so far received only first reports about the developments. From these it is evident that in the early hours of this morning Egyptian armored columns moved in an offensive thrust against Israel's borders. At the same time Egyptian planes took off from airfields in Sinai and struck out against Israel. Egyptian artillery in the Gaza Strip shelled the Israeli villages of Kissufim, Nahal-Oz and Ein Hashelosha. Netania and Kefar Yavetz have also been bombed. Israel forces engaged the Egyptians in the air and on the land, and fighting is still going on.[369]

Israel's leaders even attempted to deceive their own people by telling them that Israel was fighting to repel an Arab invasion already under way. In a radio broadcast to his people, Prime Minister Eshkol said:

> Israeli citizens: Since the early hours today our armed forces on the land and in the air have been repulsing the attack of the aggressive

---

[369] S/PV. 1347 (5 June 1967), quoted in Koch, pp. 12-13.

Egyptian forces. Egypt has imposed a military battle on us.[370]

Apparently, the Israelis were not confident that their propaganda offensive against the Arab state in the days prior to June 5 would be adequate to establish the forthcoming Israeli attack as a war of self-defense. For that reason, they supplemented their accusations by deliberately lying about who actually fired first on June 5, 1967. The Israelis, however, could not maintain for long their assertions that Egypt initiated the fighting. There were too many foreign observers in the area — journalists, U. N. observers, etc., and there was the telling fact that most of the Egyptian air force was destroyed on the ground. So, the myth of an Egyptian first strike was quickly abandoned, and Israel reverted to the assertion that although it struck first, the war was a "preemptive" one.

As it was said earlier, the Arab states had undertaken certain defensive precautions in the weeks preceding the outbreak of war on June 5 which made it possible for Israel to gain acceptance in many countries, especially in the United States, of its contention that the Arabs planned what Abba Eban described in the Security Council on the second day of the war as a "politicide, the murder of a state."[371]

---

[370] From Eshkol's broadcast on the Jerusalem Israel Domestic Service made at 1000 hours GMT, June 5, 1967, quoted in Koch, pp. 12-13.

[371] Koch, p. 13.

In May, Egypt did ask the United Nations to pull out the U. N. Emergency Force (UNEF) which was stationed on the Egyptian side of the Egypt-Israel Armistice Line since the 1956 Suez War. Egypt did place two divisions in the Sinai Peninsula. And it did blockade the Gulf of Aqaba and the Tiran Straits. But these measures were undertaken in an attempt to discourage Israel from carrying out threats to attack Syria which Israeli officials had been making in the early part of May. Such threats were so severe that the Secretary-General of the United Nations described them as being "particularly inflammatory" in a report to the Security Council made on May 19. Although threats and counter threats unfortunately had been frequent in the area, the Secretary-General said,

> In recent weeks, however, reports emanating from Israel have attributed to some high officials in that state, statements so threatening as to be particularly inflammatory in the sense that they could only heighten emotions and thereby increase tensions on the other side of the lines.[372]

Press accounts of the Israeli threats against Syria "seemed so inflammatory to U. S. State Department officials that they expressed concern to Israeli authorities."[373]

The Secretary-General of the United Nations and the U. S. State Department could afford to satisfy their apprehensions by issuing statements expressing concern

---

[372] Quoted in Charles W. Yost, "The Arab-Israeli War: How it Began," *Foreign Affairs,* January 1968, p. 309.
[373] *Ibid.*

about Israel's belligerent attitude. But the intended victims of Israeli belligerence could not afford to be satisfied with a similar verbal expression of concern. For that reason, the Egyptian government did what it thought was necessary to reduce the chances that Israel would in fact carry out its threats by going to war against Syria.

By moving two divisions into the Sinai Peninsula and by requesting the withdrawal of UNEF from the Egyptian side of the Armistice line, Egypt was, in effect, serving notice that Israel ought to reconsider its planned attack on Syria, since in the event of such an attack Israel could not be secure in the knowledge that Egypt would be a mere spectator to Israel's assault upon a sister Arab state. The closing of the Gulf of Aqaba to Israeli shipping was similarly designed to dissuade Israel from invading Syria by limiting its ability to import needed war supplies, especially oil.

Egypt made it clear that such actions were designed to deter Israeli aggression against Syria or any other Arab state. In his speech made on May 26, quoted earlier, President Nasser emphasized the deterrence motive behind his government's actions which Israel was using to prepare the world for its forthcoming "preemptive war." Publicly in his speeches, and privately in his assurances to foreign powers seeking to avert a war, President Nasser explained the defensive nature of Arab actions. Egypt would not attack first, he insisted, but Egypt would honor its defense pact with Syria if attacked, "but Israel would have to attack first."[374]

---

[374] Koch, p. 30.

Arab statements, which Israel distorted as aggressive threats, were in fact dominated by "the theme of Arab *second-strike* preparedness."[375] But Israel was determined to have its war. This determination was irrevocable in view of the fact that a diplomatic handling of the crisis, which was being made by the Security Council, would have deprived Israel of its pretext for the desired expansion. This, coupled with the dangerous belief, expressed by General Dayan in a press conference held on the first day of the war, that he could not "really remember a single important problem that was solved through diplomacy or the United Nations mediation,"[376] rendered international efforts to avert an armed conflict utterly irrelevant.

While Israel told the world that it was convinced that Egypt's request that the United Nations withdraw UNEF from the area, that its blockade of the Gulf of Aqaba, and the stationing of two divisions in the Sinai Peninsula were clear proof of Egypt's hostile intent, Israeli officials knew that such measures were not what they portrayed them to be. Israeli officials in fact admitted this much, as usual, after the event. As Israel's General Rabin conceded in an interview with the French newspaper *Le Monde*: "I do not believe that Nasser wanted war. The two divisions he sent into Sinai on May 14 would not have been enough to unleash an offensive against Israel. He

---

[375] *Ibid.*, p. 14, footnote 15.
[376] Koch, p. 17, footnote 22.

knew it and we knew it."[377] But by then, Israel had faced the world with a *fait accompli.*

Immediately after the conclusion of the war, Israel began to act in a way which leaves its expansionist designs beyond doubt. It annexed the Arab sector of Jerusalem and declared that Jerusalem was "non-negotiable." And it began to transfer Jewish populations for settlement in the occupied zones. The occupied zones were characterized as "liberated" territories reunited with the Jewish homeland.[378]

If Israel sought to avert war in 1967, why did it refuse to accede to the request of the United Nations that UNEF, being withdrawn from the Egyptian side of the Armistice Line, be re-stationed along the same lines on Israel's side? Israel had made a big issue out of President Nasser's request prior to the 1967 war that UNEF be withdrawn from Egyptian territory. It used the request to prove that Egypt had a hostile intent against Israel. If Israel believed that the presence of UNEF was a peace-keeping influence, why did it object to UNEF's continued presence by refusing to grant the U. N. permission to keep its forces along the Armistice Lines? If indeed Israel fought in self-defense, why did it find the stationing of United Nations troops between it and Egypt "entirely unacceptable?"[379]

---

[377] The interview was published in *Le Monde* on February 29, 1968, and in the Israeli paper *The Jerusalem Post* the following day. Quoted in Koch, p. 31.

[378] For a brief discussion of the incorporation of occupied Arab territories, see Koch, Chapters III and IV, pp. 33-52.

[379] Yost, p. 313.

To justify its incorporation of Arab territory, Israel contended that, prior to the 1967 war, Arab military positions on the hills surrounding Israel on the Syrian and Jordanian fronts constantly menaced Israeli villages down below, and that Israel must never again allow the return of Arab guns within firing range of Israeli settlements. In a characteristic Israeli fashion, Israeli spokesmen portrayed the alleged insecurity of Israel within its pre-war limits by comparing it to life in a concentration camp. In an interview with the West German magazine *Der Spiegel*, Abba Eban responded to a question about Israel's intention concerning the future of occupied Arab territories by saying:

> We have said very plainly the map will never again look as it did on June 4, 1967. This is a question both of security and principle for us...I don't exaggerate when I say that it reminds us of Auschwitz...the Syrians on the Golan Heights and we in the valley with the Jordanian army in sight of the coast, while the Egyptians in the Gaza Strip had their hands on our throat. This is a situation that will never occur again in history...[380]

If Israel's occupation of Arab territories was indeed motivated by a desire to free itself from this imagined Auschwitz by keeping Arab guns from returning within firing range of Israeli villages, why then is Israel building Jewish settlements in the Golan Heights and other occupied Arab lands and, thus, bringing its citizens again

---

[380] "Abba Eban Speaks Out," *Atlas*, March 1969, p. 24.

211

within the range of Arab guns? It is not inconceivable, and in view of Israel's past behavior it is not unlikely, that sometime in the near future Israel would inform the world that it would not want to reimpose upon its citizens a life in Dachau by agreeing to return to the present borders. For Israel is not yet fully grown. It has not yet reached the boundaries of "Eretz Israel."

The history of Arab-Israeli relations since the creation of Israel in 1948 indicates that it is not Israel which needs secure borders. Only people who accept uncritically Israel's sympathy-evoking story of perpetual Arab harassment see any logic in it. But those who are familiar with Israel's record as a party to the armistice and who are aware of its expansionist commitment realize that it is in fact Israel's Arab neighbors who need secure borders to "dampen 'activist' Israel's plans for further conquest."[381]

The fact cannot be overstressed that expansionism is an integral part of the concept of a Jewish state. It is not an accidental outcome of conflict, and it is not a policy adhered to today and may be renounced tomorrow. This is so because Zionism is not only an ideology which expounds the need for a Jewish state, but an ideology which purports to provide a particular solution to the "Jewish problem." And the Jewish problem is, according to Zionism, insoluble unless there exists a Jewish state capable of absorbing all the Jews of the world. Israel, the child of Zionism, is committed ideologically, legally and, one might say morally to the proposition that it must

---

[381] Hutchison, p. 96.

provide a home for the whole of world Jewry. The *raison d'etre* of Zionism and the state of Israel is to "ingather" the Jews of the world in a Jewish state. By denying entry to a Jew into "Eretz Israel" the state of Israel denies its own justification for existence.

This fact is given legal recognition by Israel in its Law of Return of 1950. which recognizes as an inherent right the right of every Jew to a place in Israel. This law was supplemented by the Nationality Act of 1952, which makes a Jew automatically a citizen upon arrival in Israel.

Israel's commitment to the "ingathering" of the Jews is illustrated by the following passage from a speech made by Golda Meir, later Prime Minister of Israel, to the United Jewish Appeal during a fund-raising tour of the United States in 1950. She said:

> Nothing is more horrifying as the discussion in which we consider whether we can keep up this pace of immigration. You have heard that immigration will have to be curtailed. I don't believe it. Don't ask me how we are going to solve it if you don't help us. But I know that there is not a single man or woman among us...who would not rue the day the state had been established, if we have to reach the decision that there is a Jew anywhere to whom we have to deny admission.[382]

This commitment to solve the "Jewish problem" by rescuing the Jews and herding them into a ghetto called

---

[382] Syrkin, pp. 252-253.

Israel serves as the propellant behind Israel's compulsive expansionism.

Friends of Israel who realize that Arab fears of Israeli expansionism have always been one of the impediments to an Arab-Israeli peace have sought to allay such Arab fears by explaining that the technical abilities of the Europeans who inhabit Israel would enable Israel to absorb a large number of people without need for territorial expansion. But how many million Jews can be crowded in the 5,600 square miles on which the United Nations decreed the establishment of a Jewish state? How many millions can live in the 8,000 square miles into which Israel grew as a consequence of its first expansion in 1947-1949?

Other friends of Israel have sought to assure the Arabs that Israel would not seek further expansion by arguing that the desire of the Israelis for a *Jewish* state would keep it from expanding, since with the acquisition of more Arab territory it would also acquire undesirable Arab populations.

> Rather than increase its Arab population, any Israeli Government will deny itself extensions of territory. Ironically enough, this exclusiveness of Israeli nationalism is the best guarantee the Arabs possess against the threat that Israel will ever launch an expansionist war.[383]

What such an assurance against Israeli expansionism ignores is the fact that Israel can expand, rid itself of the

---

[383] Crossman, *A Nation Reborn*, p. 117.

Arab population, and keep the desired land. This was in fact done in 1947-1949. As it was pointed out in Chapter 8, the Jewish state proposed by the U. N. partition resolution of 1947 did in fact contain as many Arabs as Jews. But by the time the war ended in 1949, the Israel which emerged was practically "cleansed" of Arabs and was in fact a Jewish state.

As long as Israel has the capacity to launch and win wars, Israel will continue to grow in size. This expansion will stop only if it is deterred by superior force or when the self-chosen frontiers of "Eretz Israel" are reached. Neither of these two conditions have yet been fulfilled.

CHAPTER 11 - CONCLUSIONS

> If Israel actually views a tense border as an asset
> to be exchanged for sympathetic attention and
> economic gain as if it is to be used as a
> springboard for future aggression, then a
> reappraisal of her chances of survival is long
> overdue. Israel can never aggressively fight her
> way to lasting acceptance in the Middle East.
> Commander E. H. Hutchison, *Violent Truce*

There is no evidence to suggest that any informed person seriously doubted that the partition of Palestine and the creation of a Jewish state in it could be accomplished without bloodshed. It could not have been otherwise. Injustice normally breeds conflict, and no one, not even the most ardent advocates of partition, denied that the dubious solution to the "Jewish problem" in Europe by mutilating Palestine involved an injustice against the indigenous inhabitants of the land. From the very first impartial investigation of the Zionist program, conducted by the American King-Crane Commission in 1919, it was evident that to solve the problem of a European minority group by displacing a Middle Eastern people who had done the Jews no wrong, and to inflict upon them a life of exile away from their homeland is an act of injustice.

It was the realization of this fact which impelled Herschel V. Johnson, the United States delegate to the U. N. Ad Hoc Committee on the Palestine Question, to urge his fellow delegates to support partition not on the ground that it was a just solution, but on the ground that something had to be done. "The time now is for decision," he addressed his colleagues a week before the partition resolution was passed by the General Assembly, "and work out the iniquities later on."[384]

The decision was made, but the iniquities were allowed to stand. The people of Palestine became refugees, and in their homes and on their farms came to live millions of aliens from Poland, from Russia, from Mexico, and from every other land on earth, and their only claim to the homeland of the dispossessed Palestinians was that they were of the Jewish faith.

The Palestinian people could not comprehend, let alone accept, their tragedy. In refugee camps within sight of their lost homeland, they pondered their fate. At first, it seemed like a bad dream. They could not bring themselves to believe that they, of all the nations of the earth, would not only be denied the universally conceded right of self-determination, but also the right to live in their ancestral homeland. For a while they permitted themselves to believe that soon they would be allowed to return home. That soon, someone would say: "What have these people done to deserve this?"

It became a ritual for the United Nations, in annual resolutions, to recognize the right of the Palestinians to return home. And many people around the world thought it was a pity the Palestinians suffered so much. But the Palestinians continued to be the one homeless people in

---

[384] Riggs, *Palestine in the U. N.,* pp. 55-56.

217

this world of ours. And Israel continued to "ingather" the Jews on expropriated Arab land.

In 1967, when Israel completed its conquest of Palestine, many Palestinians became refugees for the second time. They lost whatever faith they still had in the viability of the world's conscience. And they lost whatever hope they still had in the capacity of the Arab states to defend their rights. So, they resolved to try what in a lawless world remains the ultimate recourse of an oppressed people: appeal to arms. They renounced the fruitless, hopeless life of perpetual refugees and organized a movement of armed resistance to whose side the scattered Palestinians rallied in increasing numbers. Twenty years of Israel's short-sighted policy of *fait accompli* and intimidation had given it more territory, but the prize came booby-trapped, for with it came the promise of a guerilla war of indefinite duration.

The bankruptcy and short-sightedness of Israel's policy of intimidation and reliance on force are clearly seen from the fact that at the height of its military triumph, after the 1967 war, Israel experienced political and moral defeat. The United Nations General Assembly's resolution of November 22, 1967, denied Israel's right to retain the Arab territories it occupied in the June war, and left Israel's occupation standing on sheer military power. The inability of Israel to secure the cooperation of the Palestinians in the occupied territories exposed its presence as a latter-day colonial power. And the ability of the Palestine resistance movement to strike at targets which until the 1967 war were thought to be immune from guerilla attacks, like Tel Aviv and Haifa, exposed the fallacy of Israel's quest for peace and security by reliance on force.

The *fait accompli* which Israel seeks to impose in the Middle East cannot serve as a basis for a lasting settlement of the Palestine question. An attempt to perpetuate the status quo, let alone its future modification to Israel's territorial advantage, will inevitably mean perpetual conflict which can escalate into World War III. The unfitness of the status quo to be a foundation for peace stems from the very vital and central fact that the "Every step in the establishment of a Zionist state had been a challenge to justice."[385]

No solution to Palestine's problem which envisions the perpetual exclusion of the Palestinian Arab people from their homeland is likely to survive. Even if Israel does succeed into bludgeoning the Arab states into acquiescing in such a solution, an unlikely prospect, it will never be able to persuade the Palestinians of the legitimacy of the "Only Jews Allowed" signs that Israel displays along its "borders." The Zionists, who successfully capitalized on an alleged yearning of the Jewish people for a land they never saw, must be the first to understand the Palestinian Arab's yearning for this same land that has been the only land they ever knew.

It is conceivable, of course, that Israel may choose to reconcile itself to a self-inflicted status of a super-ghetto in constant conflict with its environment. It is possible that the Zionist leaders of Israel really share the belief of Theodor Herzl, their ideological godfather, that

---

[385] Hutchison, p. 95.

"Universal brotherhood is not even a beautiful dream. Antagonism is essential to man's greatest efforts."[386]

Unfortunately, there does seem to exist a possibility that this fatal state of mind is in fact taking root in Israel. On the basis of his experiences as Chief of Staff of UNTSO and, later, commander of the U. N. Emergency Force in the Middle East, Lieutenant-General Burns expressed these apprehensions as follows:

> It is not unreasonable to deduce that a society whose young elements have passed their most formative years in an atmosphere in which the military virtues and especially aggressiveness are given the highest values, and where the Arab is always the enemy, to be made to submit to Israel's demands by ruthless force, will be increasingly militaristic and less inclined to the solving by negotiation of external problems...And so, born of the success of the campaigns of 1948 and 1956, there is a certain arrogance, and inability to see that Israel should yield anything for peace, an inability to compromise. Such an attitude in what will soon be the majority of the population does not promise a peaceful solution of Israel's problems, or a peaceful future for the Middle East.[387]

This dismal future is the only option to which the Zionist solution to the "Jewish problem" leads. The Zionist insistence that no Jew is safe among Gentiles and

---

[386] Herzl, *The Jewish State*, p. 153.

[387] Burns, p. 68. This view was shared by other U. N. observers in Palestine. See Hutchison, p. 142.

that all Jews must be "ingathered" in a Jewish state inevitably leads Israel to continue to refuse to recognize the right of the Arabs of Palestine to return to their country and to propel Israel toward further expansionism The implications of Israel's Zionism are, therefore, clear and they point to perpetual conflict with deadly certainty. Zionism leaves no practical alternative is sight.

The only way for Arabs and Jews to coexist in Palestine is to do precisely that: to *coexist*. The *displacement* of one people to accommodate the other's yearning for a home would never do. A Palestinian state, in which all *Palestinians*, Arabs and Jews, can live is an essential prerequisite for peace in the Middle East. The Arab people have always been prepared to coexist with Jews in Palestine as well as in other Arab territories. The Arabs have never indulged in anti-Semitism, have never persecuted Jews, and have never denied them entry into Arab lands. What the Arabs object to is the exclusiveness of Zionist "nationalism" which does not reciprocate this tolerance.

The Arabs' willingness to coexist is demonstrated by the fact that they did not object to Jewish immigration into Palestine until it became apparent that the Zionists were not coming in search of a home alongside the native inhabitants of the country but to force them out of the country into a life of exile.[388] It is further demonstrated by the fact that, even now after experiencing decades of undeserved suffering, the Palestinian Arabs seek no more than the right to live with other Palestinians of whatever

---

[388] See Chapter 5.

faith in a free, secular Palestine. The Palestinian resistance movement has repeatedly proclaimed that its objectives do not include and never did include the Zionist-inspired stories of Arab determination to "throw the Jews into the sea," and sought nothing more than the assertion of the equal right of the Palestinian Arabs to live on equal terms in binational Palestinian state.[389]

This commitment to coexistence is not a slogan adopted by the leaders of the Palestine resistance movement to gain sympathy for its cause. It is a goal for which it strives and an attitude which it seeks to inculcate in Palestinian children in refugee camps. A writer who visited training camps of Palestinian Arab commando organizations in Jordan reported that he found these organizations consciously teaching their recruits as well as the Palestinian children in refugee camps that they must be prepared for a future when they are co-citizens with the Jews in a free state of Palestine, and that to this end "the children are taught to distinguish between Jewishness and Zionism."[390] It is not the Jews to whom the Arabs have sworn enmity, but to the Zionist state which is blind to the rights of non-Jews[391]. Is the concept of a free,

---

[389]" The Palestinian Resistance," *Fatah* (a periodical publication of The Palestine Liberation Organization), April 16, 1969, p. 5.

[390] Patrick Marnham, "In Secret Camps in Jordan, Palestinian guerillas train for war against Israel," *Weekend Magazine*, April 26, 1969.

[391]Editor's note: The official position of Palestine changed to the two-state solution with the Oslo Accords. On Sept. 29, 2024, the foreign minister of Jordan announced a Muslim and Arab Committee of 57 countries guaranteed the security of Israel if a sovereign Palestinian state was established along the June 4, 1967 borders. https://www.youtube.com/watch?v=GYr3hYjHIx8.

binational Palestinian state an idle dream, or is it a hopeful solution to Palestine's problem? If the Jews came to Palestine to live, then it is a solution. But if they came to Palestine to conquer, then it must remain a dream. With the Zionists rests this fateful choice. And on their choice depends the type of tomorrow which will dawn on the sacred soil of Palestine.

SELECTED BIBLIOGRAPHY

"Abba Eban Speaks Out," *Atlas*, March 1969, pp. 22-24.

Abed, Ibrahim, Al-, *The Mapai: The Governing Party in Israel*. Palestine Monographs no. 7. Research Center, Palestine Liberation Organization. Beirut, 1966. (In Arabic).

_____, *Violence and Peace: A Study of Zionist Strategy*. Palestine Monographs no. 10. Research Center, Palestine Liberation Organization. Beirut, 1967. (In Arabic).

Anati, Emmanuel, *Palestine Before the Hebrews*. New York: Alfred P. Knopf, 1963.

Antonius, George, *The Arab Awakening*. New York: G. P. Putnam's Sons, 1946.

Balfour, Earl of, *Opinions and Arguments From Speeches and Addresses of the Earl of Balfour, 1910-1927*. Garden City, New York: Doubleday, Doran & Co., Inc., 1928.

Begin, Menachem, *The Revolt: Story of the Irgun*. New York: Henry Schuman, Inc., 1951.

Ben Gurion, David, "The Call of Spirit in Israel," State of Israel, *Government Yearbook*, 1951-52, pp. vii-xlvi.

_____, "Israel Among the Nations," State of Israel, *Government Yearbook*, 1952, pp. 1-47.

_____, *Israel: Years of Challenge*. New York: Holt, Rinehart and Winston, 1963.

_____, "Jewish Survival," State of Israel, *Government Yearbook*, 1953-54, pp. 1-50.
_____, *Rebirth and Destiny of Israel*. New York: Philosophical Library, 1954.

Brilliant, Moshe, "Israel's Policy of Reprisals," *Harper's Magazine*, March, 1955, pp. 68-72.

Brook, David, *Preface to Peace: The United Nations and the Arab-Israeli Armistice System*. Washington, D. C.: Public Affairs Press, 1964.

Burns, Lt. General E. L. M., *Between Arab and Israeli*. New York: Ivan Obolensky, Inc., 1962.

Childers, Erskine B., "The Other Exodus," *The Spectator*, May 12, 1961, pp. 672-675.

Cooke, Hedley V., *Israel: A Blessing and a Curse*. London: Stevens & Sons Ltd., 1960.

Crossman, Richard H. S., *A Nation Reborn*. New York: Atheneum Publishers, 1960.

_____, *Palestine Mission: A Personal Record*. New York: Harper & Brothers, 1947.

Crum, Bartley C., *Behind the Silken Curtain*, New York : Simon and Schuster, 1947.

Derfler, Leslie, *The Dreyfus Affairs Tragedy of Errors?* Boston: D. C. Heath and Co., 1963.

Draper, Theodore, *Israel and World Politics: Roots of the Third Arab-Israeli War*, New York: The Viking Press, 1968.

Dugdale, Blanche E. C., *Arthur James Balfour*. 2 volumes. New York: G. P. Putnam's Sons, 1937.

Frank, Waldo, *Bridgehead: The Drama of Israel*. New York: George Braziller, Inc., 1957.

Garcia-Granados, Jorge, *The Birth of Israel*. New York: Alfred A. Knopf, 1948.

Ghazaleh, Bassam Abu, *The Terrorist Roots of the Israeli Herut Party*. Palestine Monographs no. 5. Research Center, Palestine Liberation Organization. Beirut, 1966. (In Arabic).

Glubb, Sir John Bagot, *A Soldier With the Arabs*. New York : Harper & Brothers Publishers, 1957.

Gottheil, Richard J. H., *Zionism*. Philadelphia: The Jewish Publication Society of America, 1939.

Halasz, Nicholas, *Captain Dreyfus: The Story of a Mass Hysteria*, New York: Grove Press, 1955.

Halpern, Ben, *The Idea of the Jewish State*. Cambridge, Mass.: Harvard University Press, 1961.

Handlin, Oscar, *The American People in the Twentieth Century*. Cambridge, Mass.: Harvard University Press, 1954.

Hanna, Paul L., *British Policy in Palestine*. Washington, D. C.: American Council on Public Affairs, 1942.

Heller, Joseph, *The Zionist Idea*. New York: Schocken Books, 1949.

Herzl, Theodor, *The Jewish State*. New York : American Zionist Emergency Council, 1946.

Howard, Harry N., *The King-Crane Commission*. Beirut: Khayats, 1963.

Hutchison, Commander E. H., *Violent Truce*. New York: TheDevin-Adair Co., 1956.

Iskandar, Marwan. *The Arab Boycott of Israel*. Palestine Monographs no. 6. Research Center, Palestine Liberation Organization. Beirut, 1966. (In English).

Jabara, Abdeen M., *The Armistice in International Law*. Palestine Monographs no. 2. Research Center, Palestine Liberation Organization. Beirut, 1966. (In English).

Jiryes, Sabri, *The Arabs in Israel*. Palestine Monographs no. 14. Research Center, Palestine Liberation Organization. Beirut, 1967. (In Arabic).

Joseph, Bernard, *British Rule in Palestine*. Washington, D. C.: Public Affairs Press, 1948.

Joseph, Dov, *The Faithful City: The Siege of Jerusalem, 1948.* New York: Simon and Schuster, 1960.

Katz, Samuel, *Days of Fire.* Garden City, New York: Doubleday & Co., Inc., 1968.

Kayyali, Abd Al-Wahab, *The Kibbutz, or the Collectivist Farm in Israel.* Palestine Monographs no. 4. Research Center, Palestine Liberation Organization. Beirut, 1966. (In Arabic).

_____, *Zionist Expansionist Ambitions.* Palestine Monographs no. 3. Research Center, Palestine Liberation Organization. Beirut, 1966. (In Arabic).

Kedward, H. R., *The Dreyfus Affair: Catalyst for Tensions in French Society.* London: Longmans, Green and Co. Ltd., 1965.

Key, V. O., *Politics, Parties, and Pressure Groups.* New York: Thomas Y. Crowell Co., 1948.

Khouri, Fred J., *The Arab-Israeli Dilemma.* Syracuse, New York: Syracuse University Press, 1968.

_____, "The Policy of Retaliation in Arab-Israeli Relations," *The Middle East Journal,* (Autumn, 1966), pp. 435-455.

Kimche, Jon and David, *The Secret Roads.* New York: Farrar, Straus and Cudahy, Inc., 1955.

Koch, Howard, Jr., *Six Hundred Days: A Reappraisal of the Arab-Israeli Confrontation Since June, 1967.* New

York: Permanent Observer of the League of Arab States to the United Nations, March, 1969.

Lilienthal, Alfred. *There Goes the Middle East*. New York: The Bookmailer, Inc., 1961.

_____, *What Price Israel?* Chicago: Henry Regnery Co., 1953.

Lorch, Netanel, *The Edge of the Sword: Israel's War of Independence, 1947-1949*. New York: G. P. Putnam's Sons, 1961.

Louis, William Roger, "The United Kingdom and the Beginning of the Mandates System, 1919-1922," *International Organization*, XXIII (Winter, 1969), pp. 73-96.

Lowenthal, Marvin (ed.), *The Diaries of Theodor Herzl*. New York: The Dial Press, 1956.

McDonald, James G., *My Mission in Israel, 1948-1951*. New York: Simon and Schuster, 1951.

Marlowe, John, *Rebellion in Palestine*. London: The Cresset Press, 1946.

_____, *The Seat of Pilate: An Account of the Palestine Mandate*. London: The Cresset Press, 1959.

Mehdi, M. T., *Kennedy and Sirhan, Why?* New York: New World Press, 1968.

Millis, Walter (ed.), *The Forrestal Diaries*. New York: The Viking Press, 1951.

Nasser, Gamal Abd El-, *The Philosophy of the Revolution*. Cairo: Dar Al-Ma'aref, n. d.

Nordau, Max and Gottheil, Gustav, *Zionism and Anti-Semitism*. New York: Fox, Duffield & Co., 1905.

Nutting, Anthony, *The Arabs*. New York: The American Library, 1964.

_____, *I Saw For Myself: The Aftermath of Suez*. Garden City, New York: Doubleday and Co., Inc., 1958.

Peretz, Don, "The Arab Minority of Israel," *The Middle East Journal*, VIII (Spring, 1954), pp. 139-154.
_____, "Problems of Arab Refugee Compensation," *The Middle East Journal*, VIII (Autumn, 1954), pp. 403-416.

Qadi, Laila Al-, *The Histadrut*. Palestine Monographs no. 9.Research Center, Palestine Liberation Organization. Beirut, 1967. (In Arabic).

Rahman, As'ad Abd Ar-, *Israeli Penetration in Asia: India and Israel*. Palestine Monographs no. 11. Research Center, Palestine Liberation Organization. Beirut, 1967. (In Arabic).

_____, *The World Zionist Organization: Its Structure and Work, 1897-1948*. Palestine Monographs no. 15. Research Center, Palestine Liberation Organization. Beirut, 1967. (In Arabic).

Razouk, Assad, *A Look at Israeli Parties.* Palestine Monographs no. 8. Research Center, Palestine Liberation Organization. Beirut, 1968. (In Arabic).

Riggs, Robert E., *Politics in the United Nations.* Urbana, Illinois: University of Illinois Press, 1958.

Ro'i, Yaacov, "The Zionist Attitude to the Arabs, 1908-1914," *Middle Eastern Studies,* IV (April, 1968), pp. 200-235.

Royal Institute of International Affairs. *Great Britain and Palestine, 1915-1945.* London: Oxford University Press, 1946.

Rushdi, Omar, *Zionism and Its Protégé Israel.* Cairo: Maktabat An-Nahda Al-Masriya, 1965. (In Arabic).

Sacher, Harry, *Israel: The Establishment of a State.* London: George Weidenfeld & Nicolson, 1952.

Sayegh, Anees, *The Balance of Military Power Between the Arab States and Israel.* Palestine Monographs No. 12. Research Center, Palestine Liberation Organization. Beirut, 1967. (In Arabic).

Sayegh, Fayez, *The Arab-Israeli Conflict.* New York: The Arab Information Center, 1956.

_____, *The Record of Israel at the United Nations.* New York: The Arab Information Center, 1957.

_____, *Zionist Colonialism in Palestine.* Palestine Monographs no. 1. Research Center, Palestine Liberation Organization. Beirut, 1965. (In Arabic).

_____, *Zionist Diplomacy*. Palestine Monographs no. 13. Research Center, Palestine Liberation Organization. Beirut, 1967. (In Arabic).

Schwarz Walter, *The Arabs in Israel*. London: Faber and Faber, 1959.

Stein, Leonard, *The Balfour Declaration*. New York: Simon and Schuster, 1961.

Syrkin, Marie, *Golda Meir: Woman With a Cause*. New York: G. P. Putnam's Sons, 1963.

Third Force Movement in Israel. *A Voice From Israel Demanding Justice for the Arabs*.

Tomeh, George J., "Challenge and Response: A Judgment of History," The Arab World, XV (May, 1969), pp. 13-14.

Toynbee, Arnold, *A Study of History*. Vol. VIII. London: Oxford University Press, 1954.

Tuchman, Barbara W., *The Proud Tower*. New York: Macmillan, 1966.

United Nations, Commissioner of UNRWA, *1967 Report*.

Utley, Freda, *Will the Middle East Go West?* Chicago: Henry Regnery Co., 1957.

Von Horn, Major General Carl, *Soldiering for Peace*. New York: David McKay Co., 1967.

Weizmann, Chaim, *Trial and Error.* New York : Harper & Brothers, 1949.

Welles, Sumner, *We Need Not Fail.* Boston: Houghton Mifflin Co., 1948.

ABOUT THE AUTHOR

1932-2017

Muhammad Hallaj, a political scientist specializing in Palestinian affairs and the Israeli-Palestinian conflict, was born in Qalqilya, Palestine. After earning his doctorate from the University of Florida in 1966, he taught at Florida's Jacksonville University and then at the University of Jordan in Amman. Hallaj returned to the West Bank in 1975, where he served as dean of social sciences and later as academic vice president of Birzeit University before becoming the first director of the Council for Higher Education in the West Bank and Gaza. While taking a leave to go to Harvard University as a visiting scholar in 1983, Hallaj was denied a visa to return to the West Bank. Among the positions he has held since then have been editor of Palestine Perspectives (1983–1991), member (and subsequent head) of the Palestinian delegation on Refugees to the multilateral peace talks following the Madrid conference (1991–1993), and executive director of the Palestine Center and the Jerusalem Fund. He also served for many years on the board of the Independent Palestinian Commission for Citizens' Rights.